RanSom StyLE Letters

Cutout & Collage BOOK

Contents

Published by Fresh Type Books

First Edition: Jan 2026
Printed in the United States of America

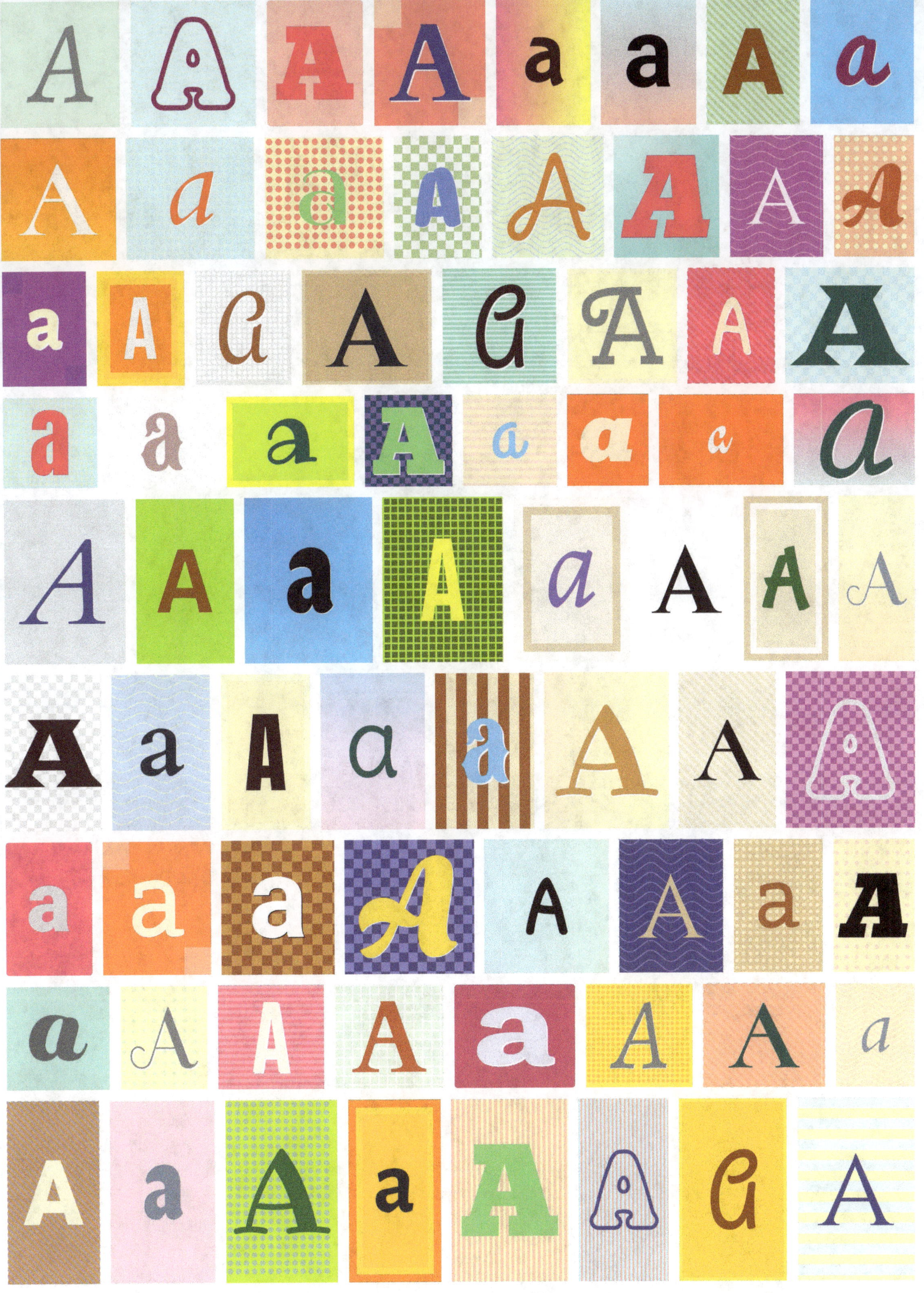

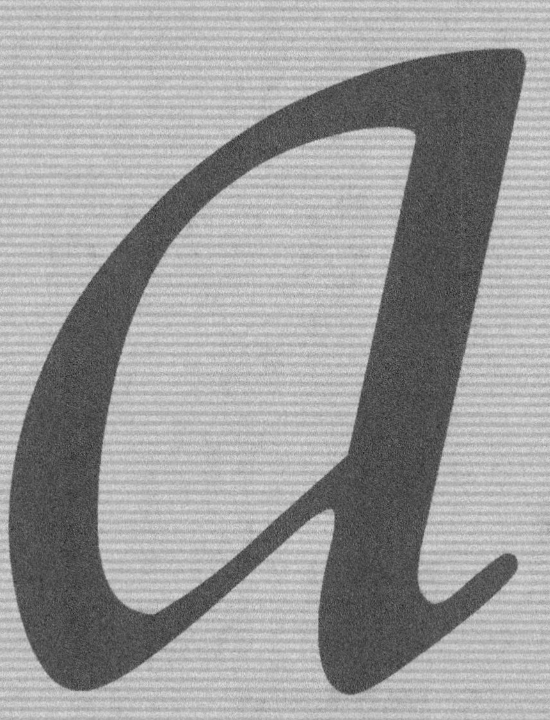

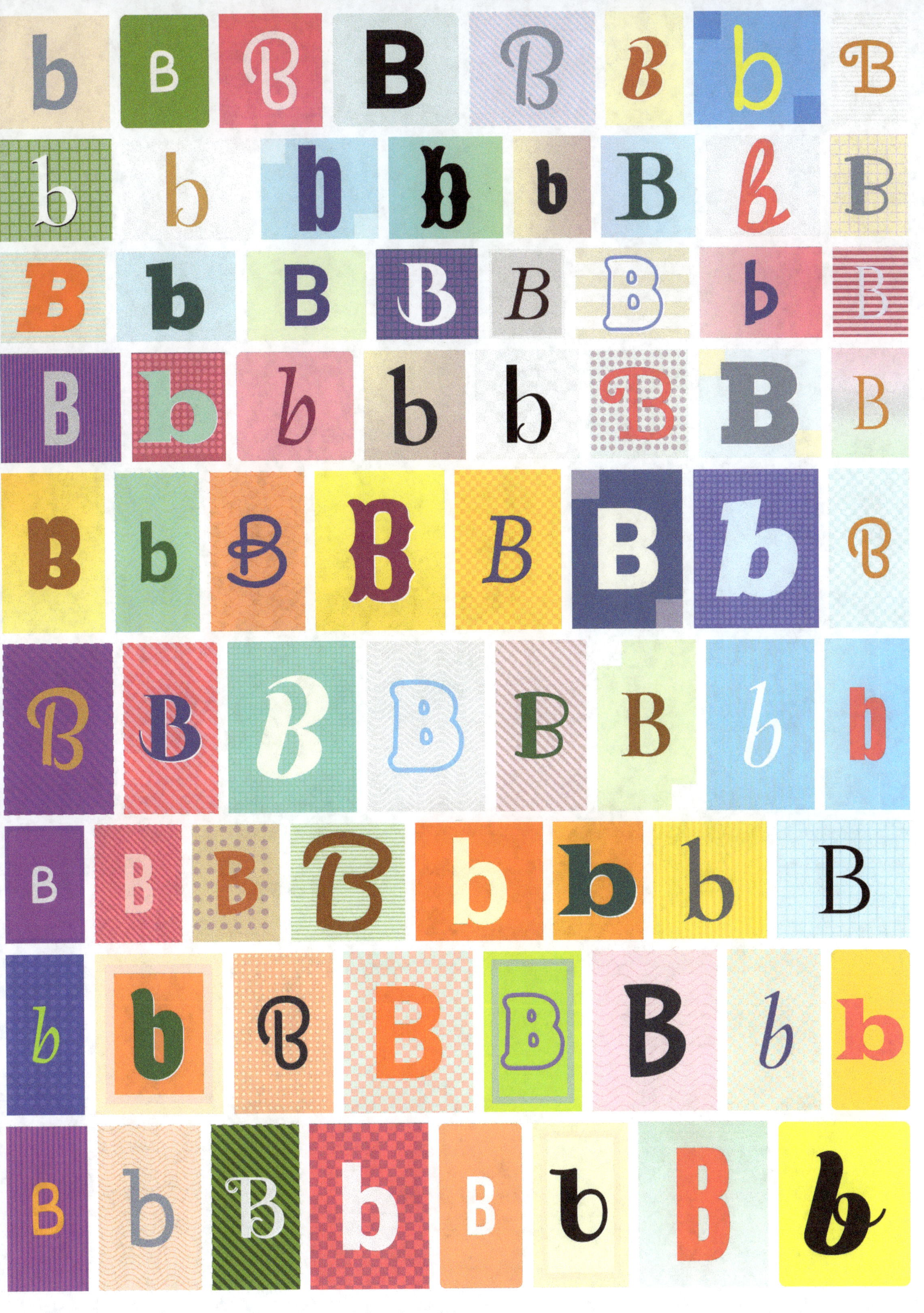

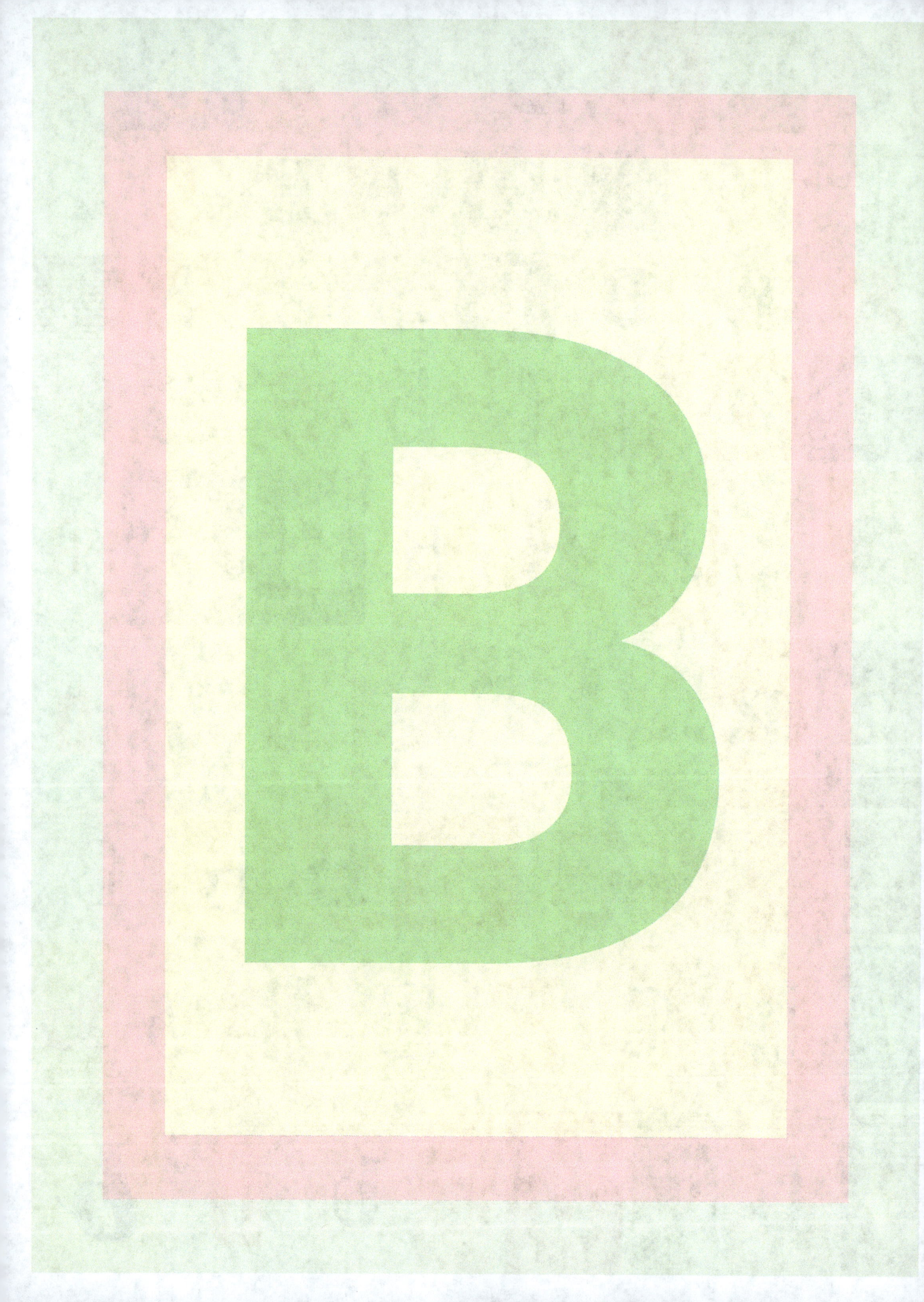

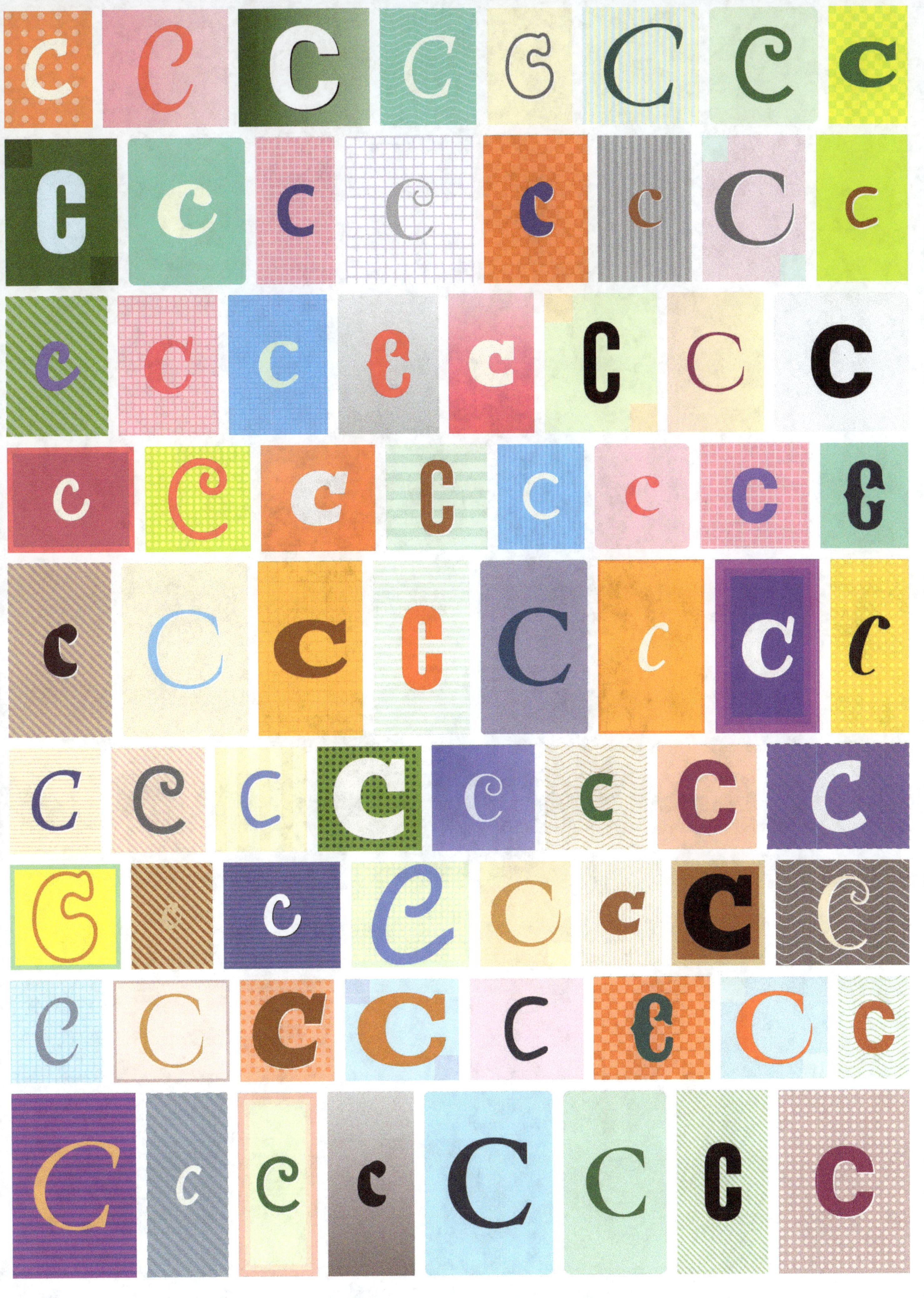

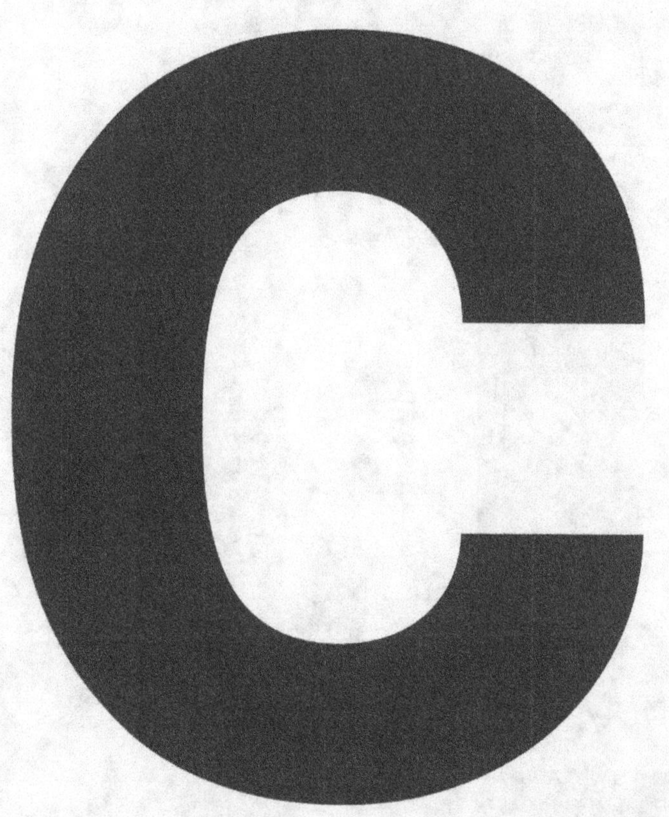

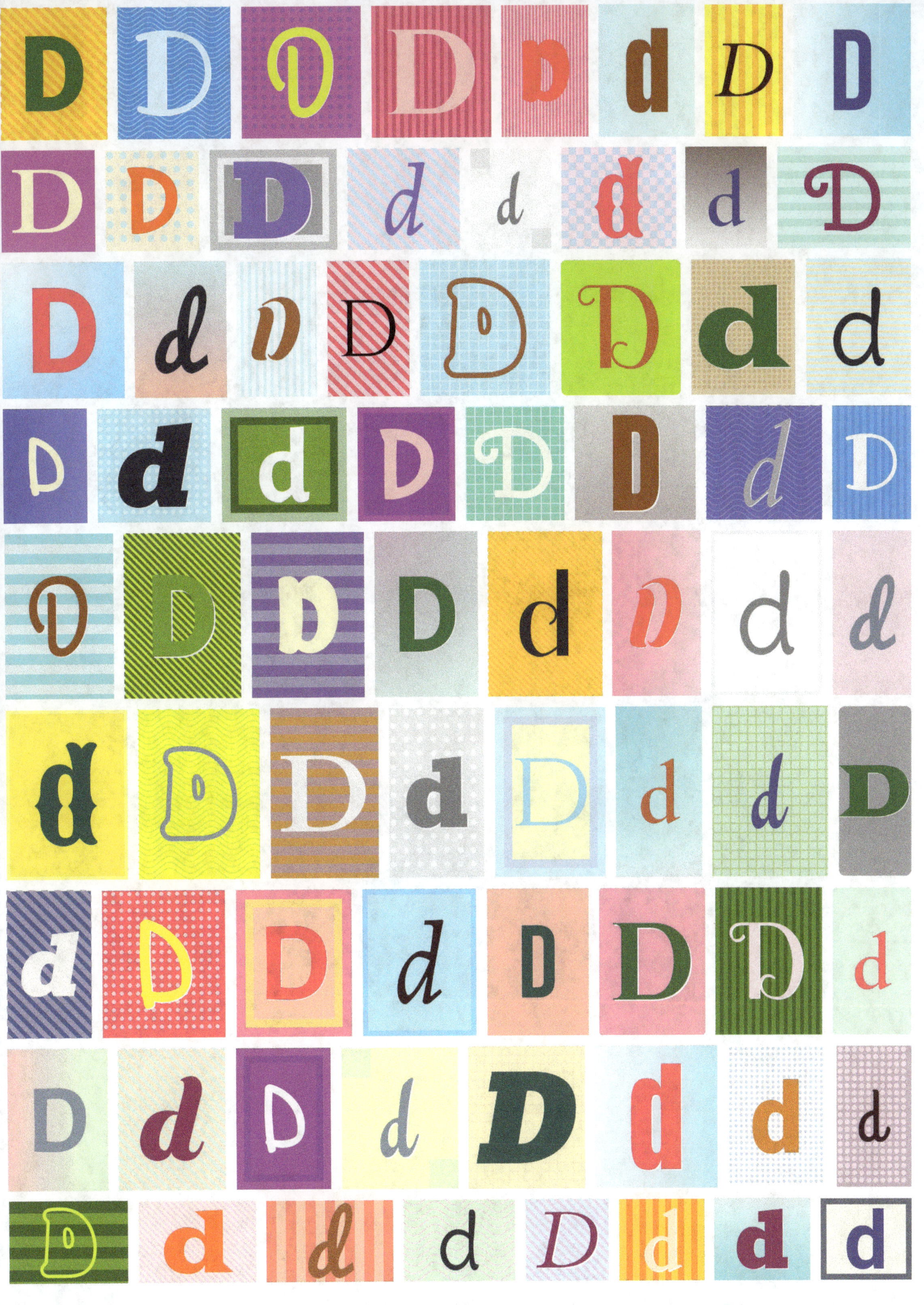

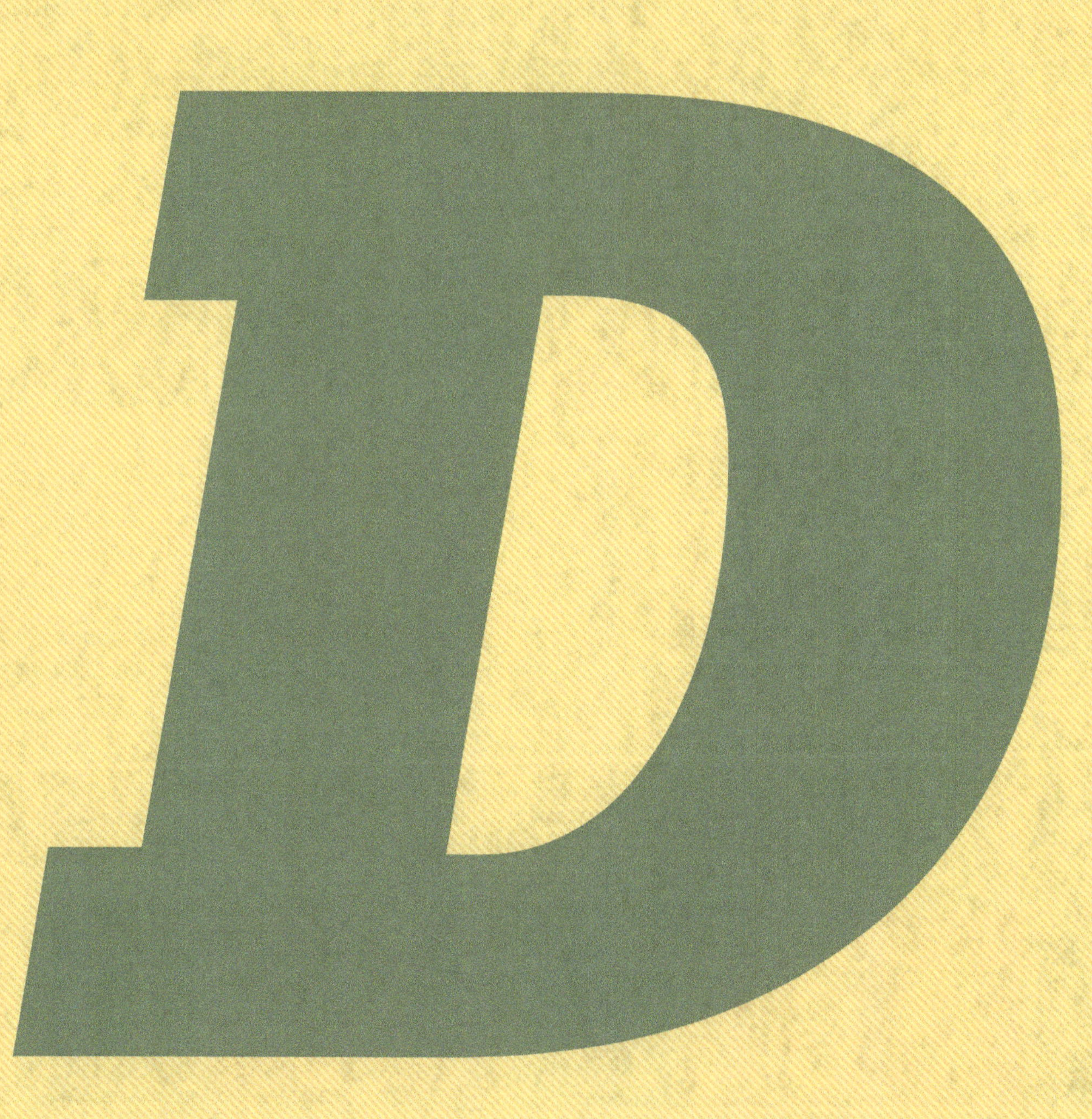

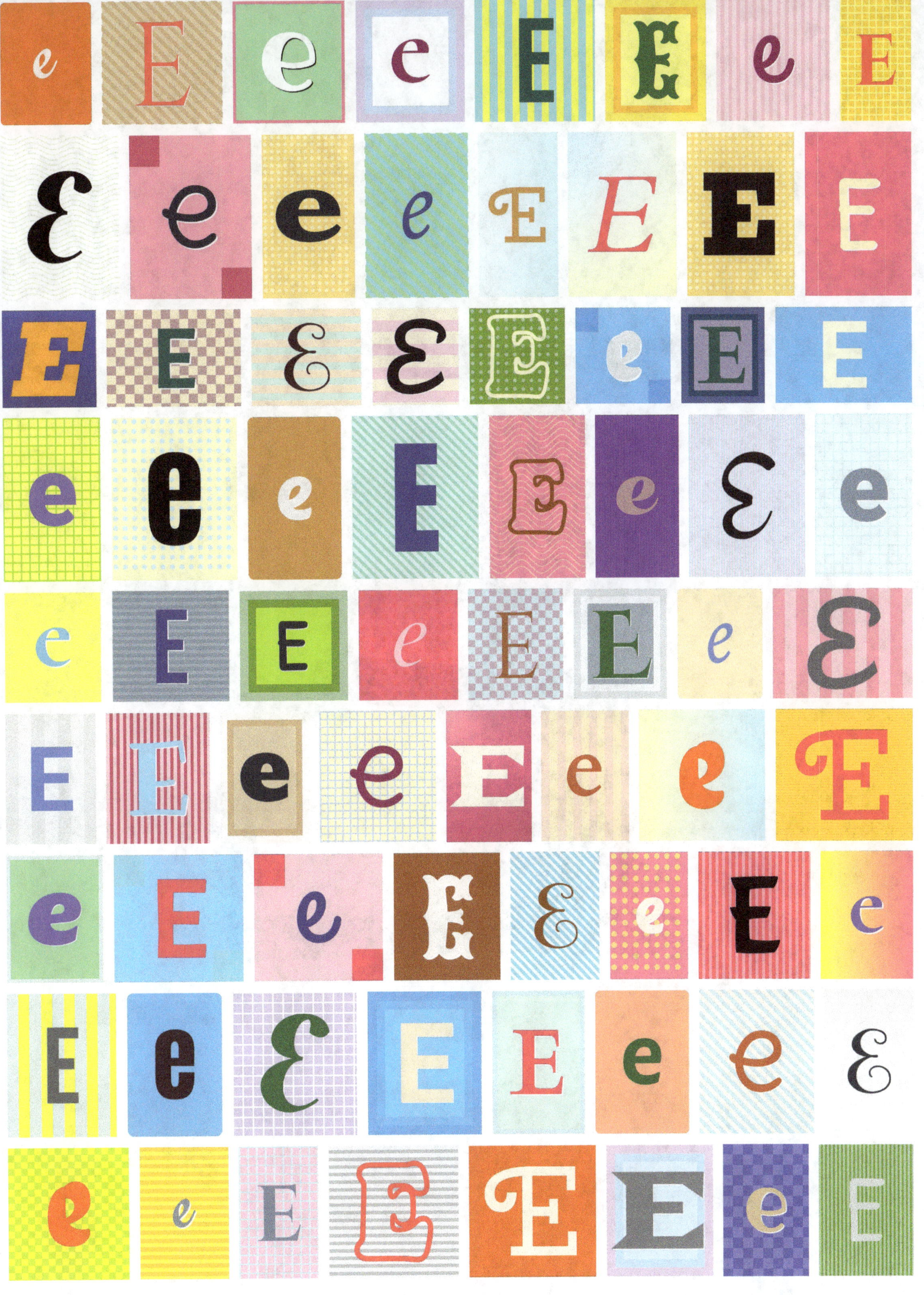

E

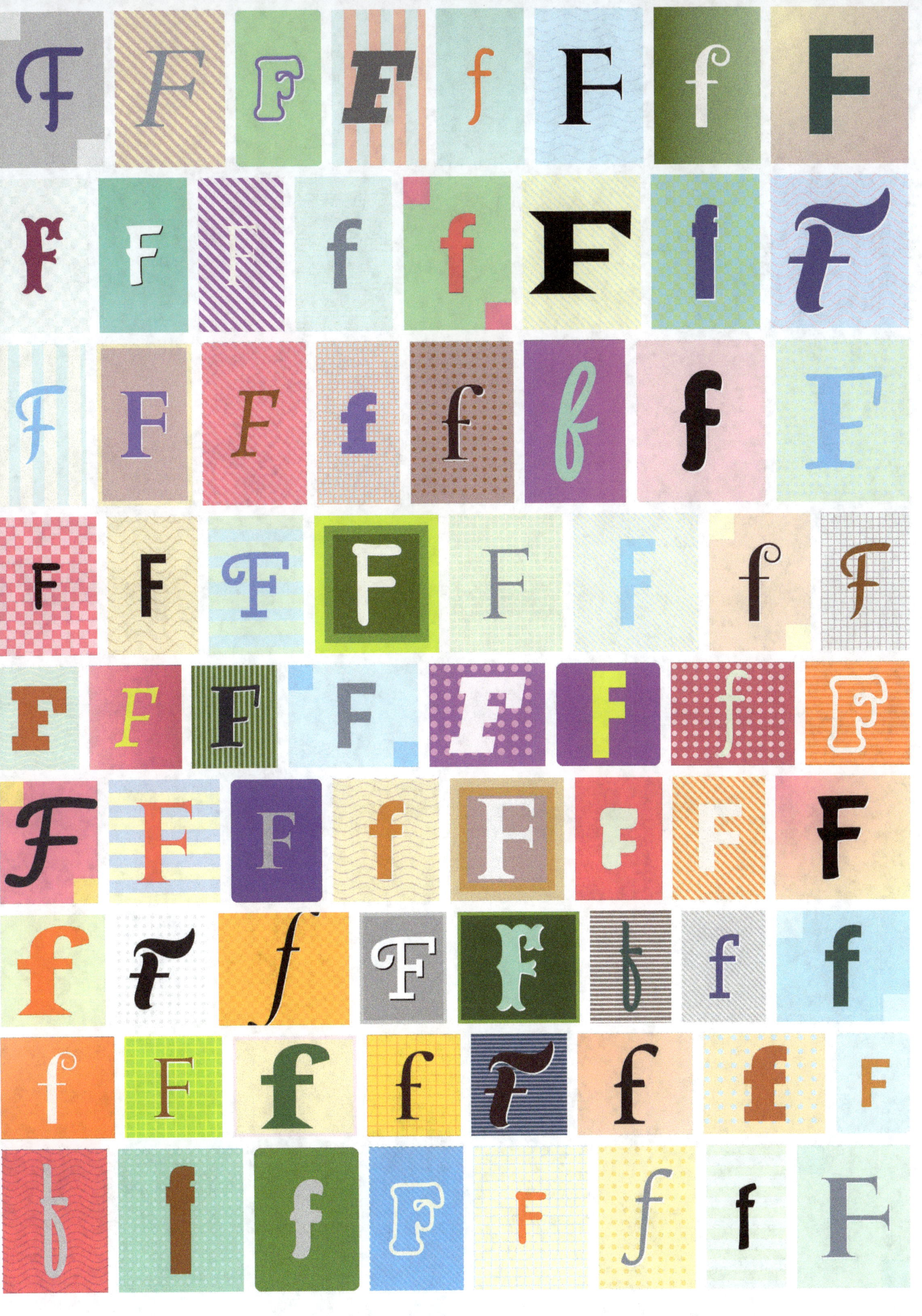

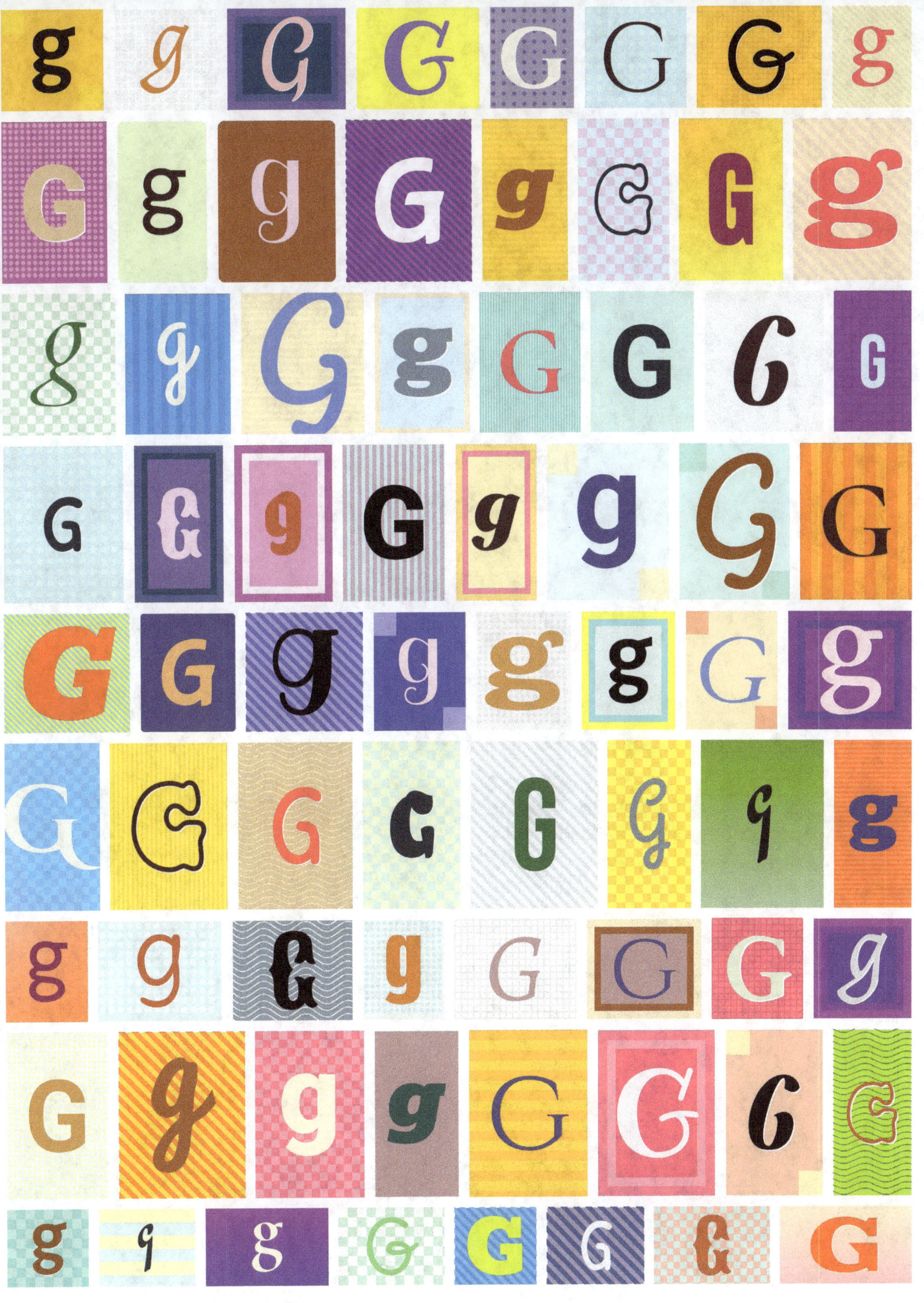

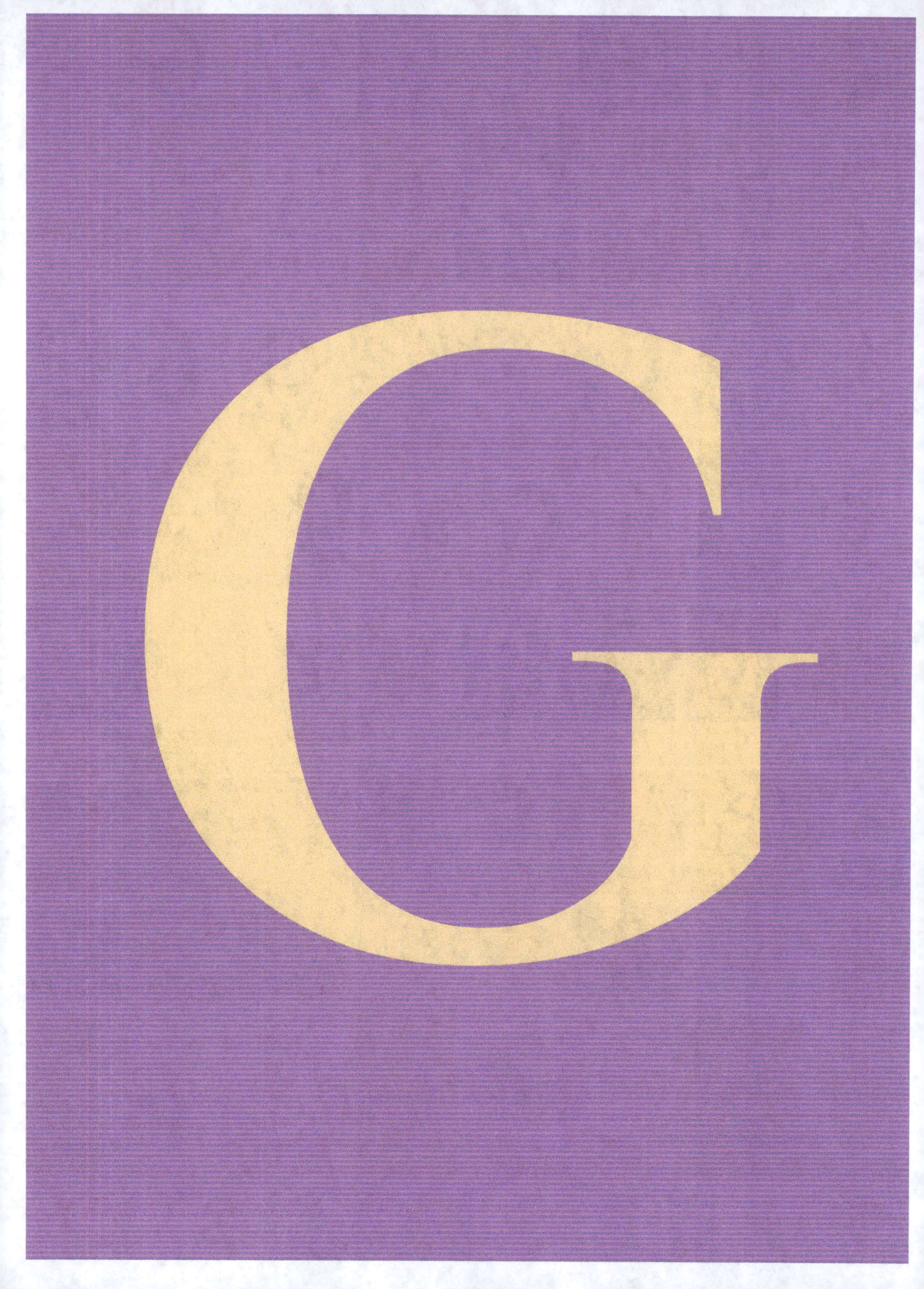

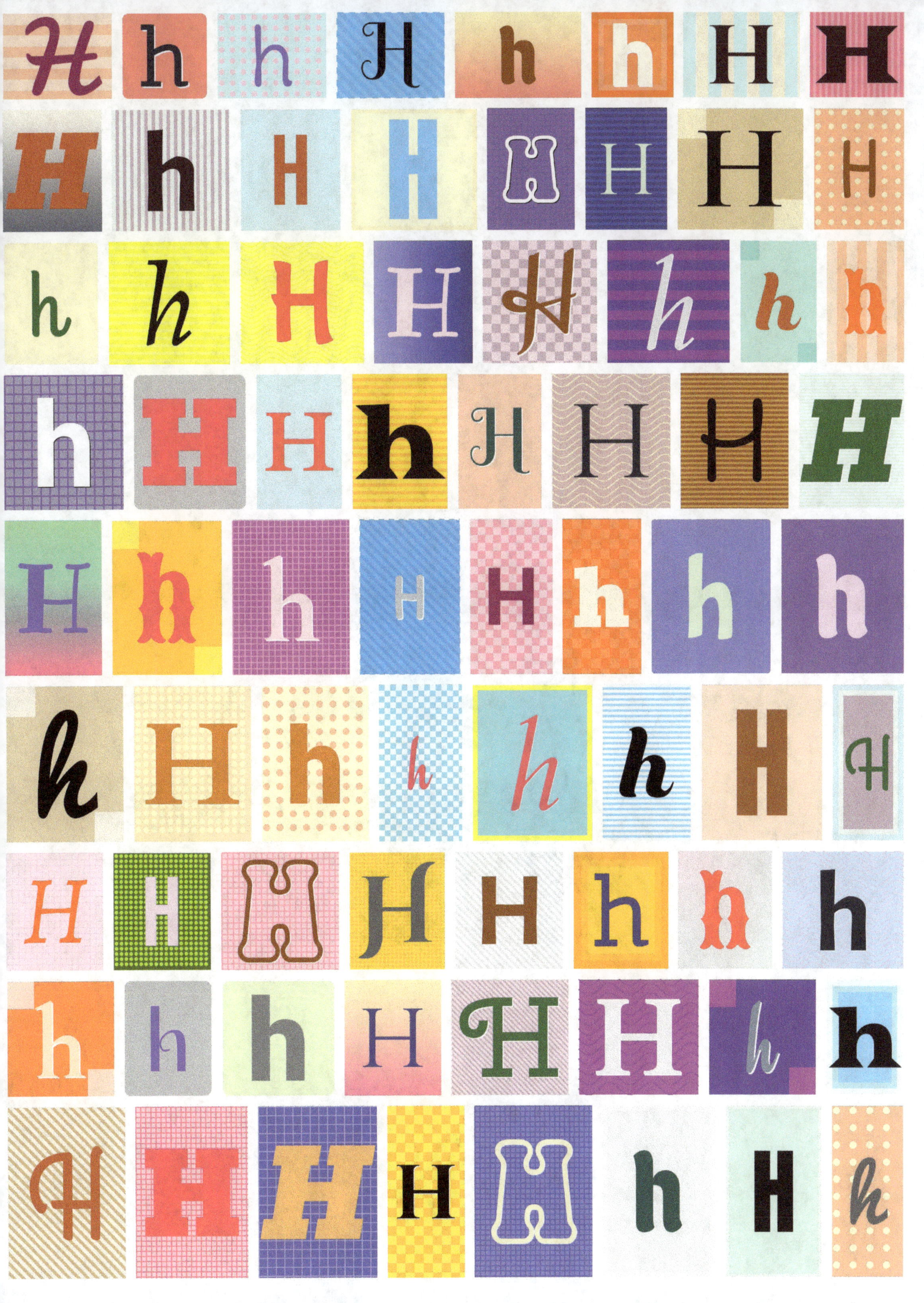

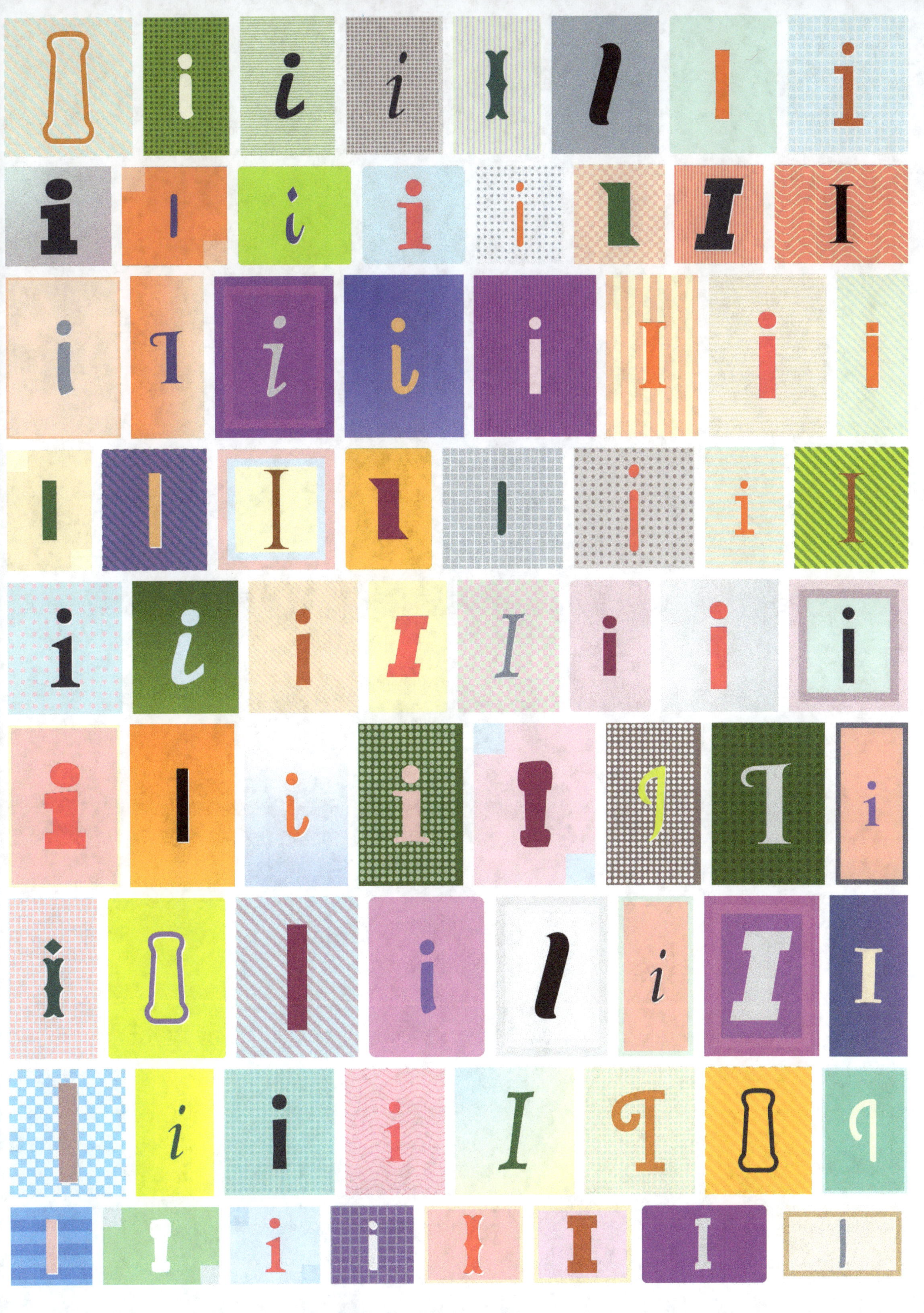

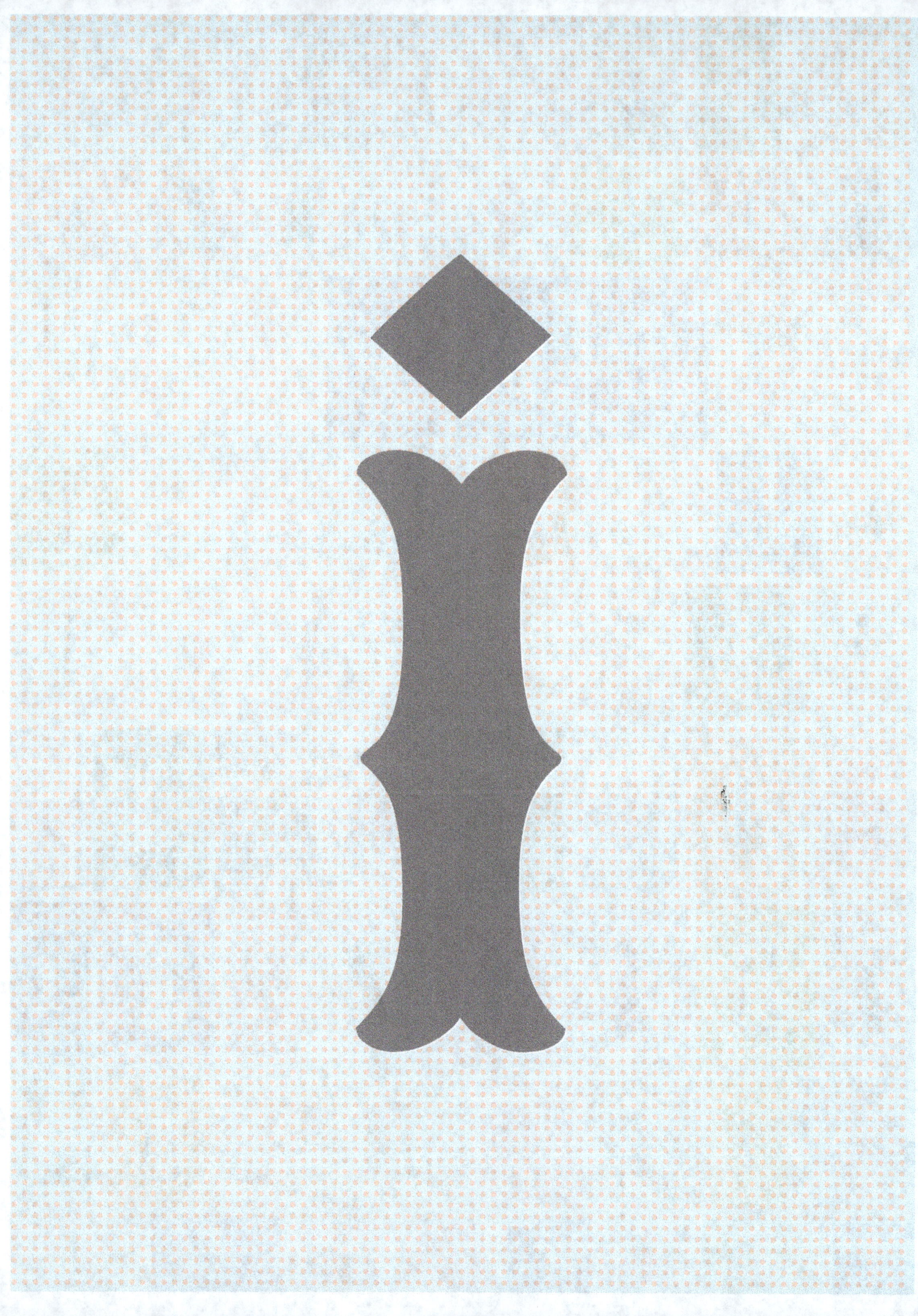

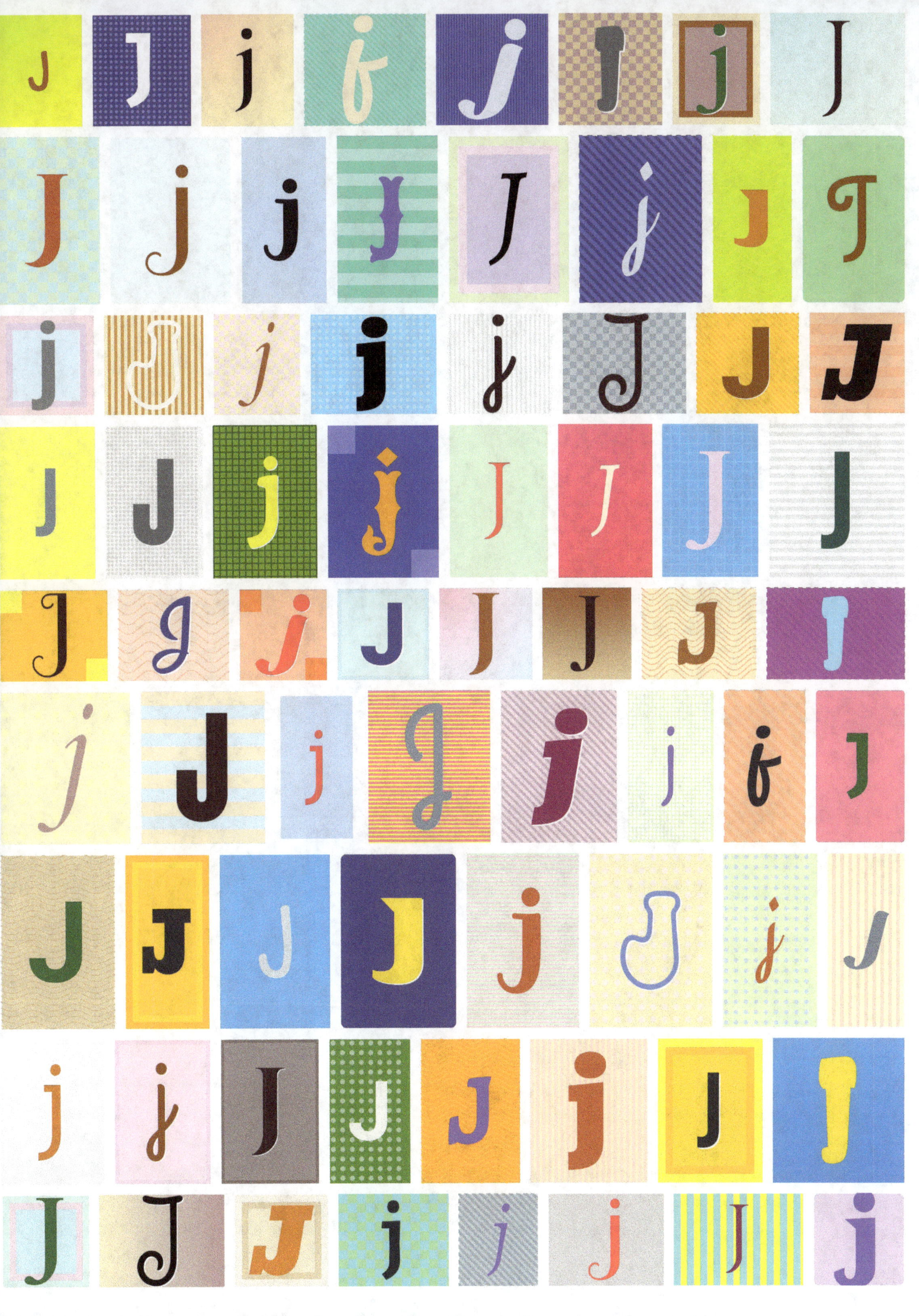

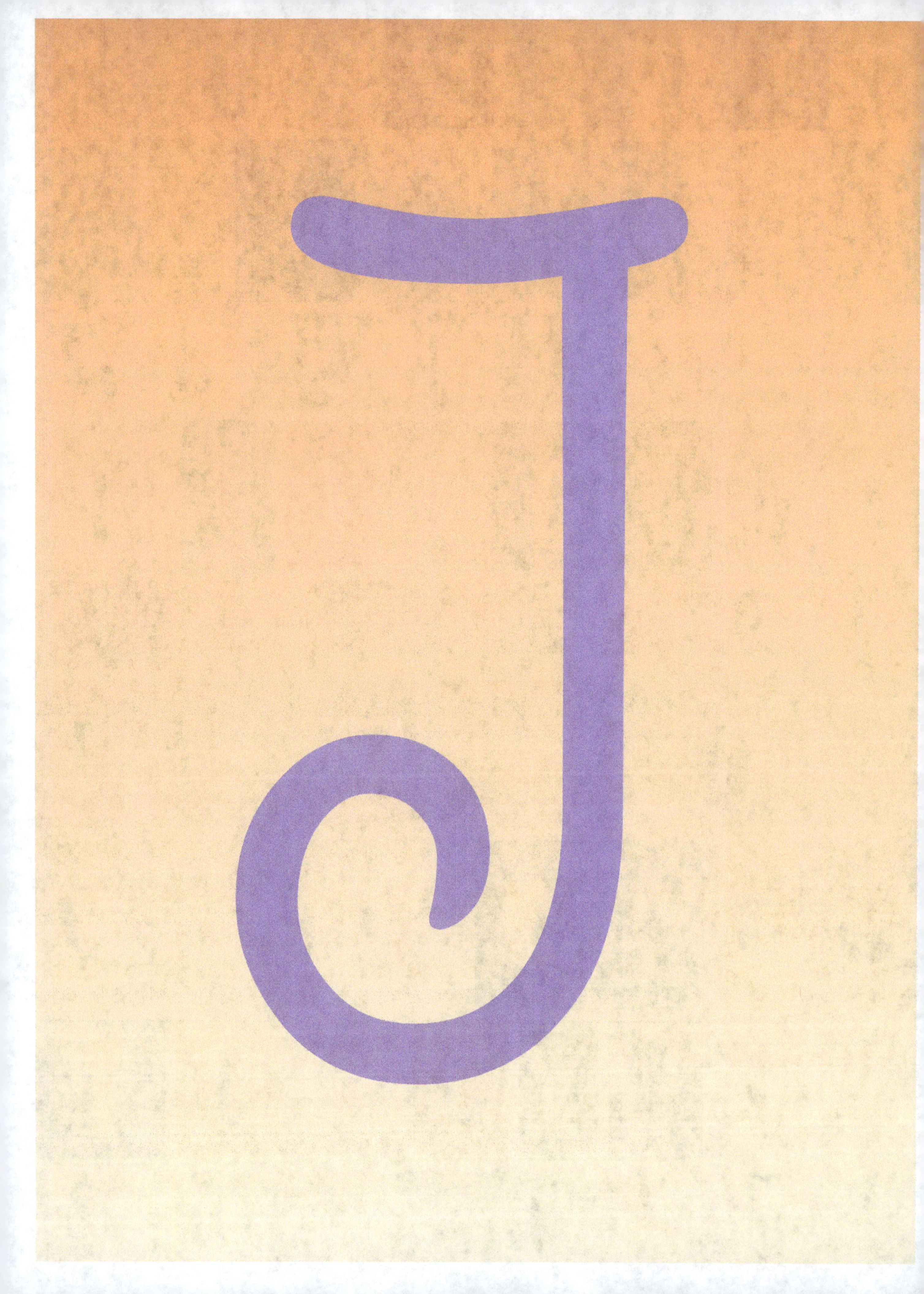

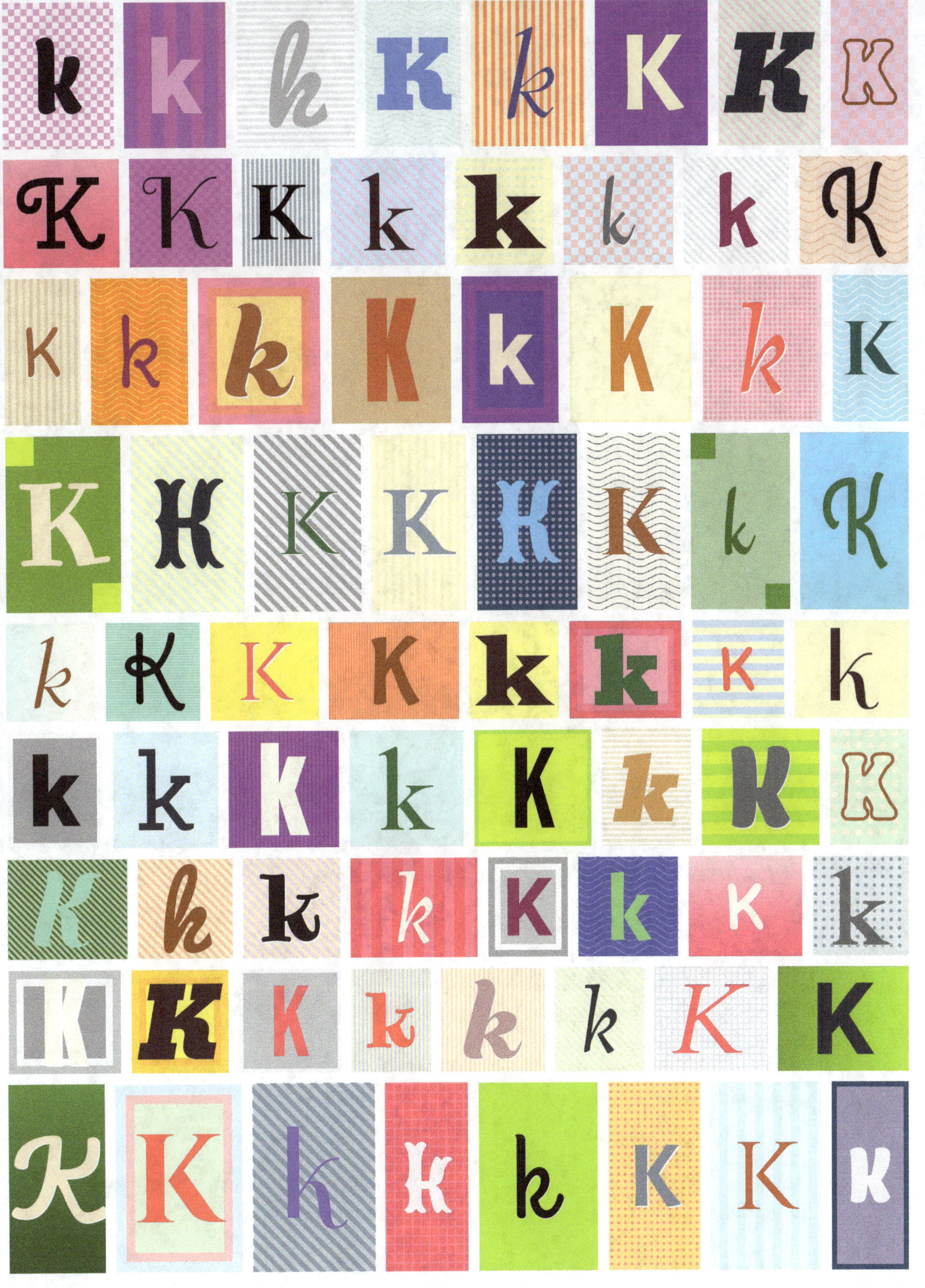

K

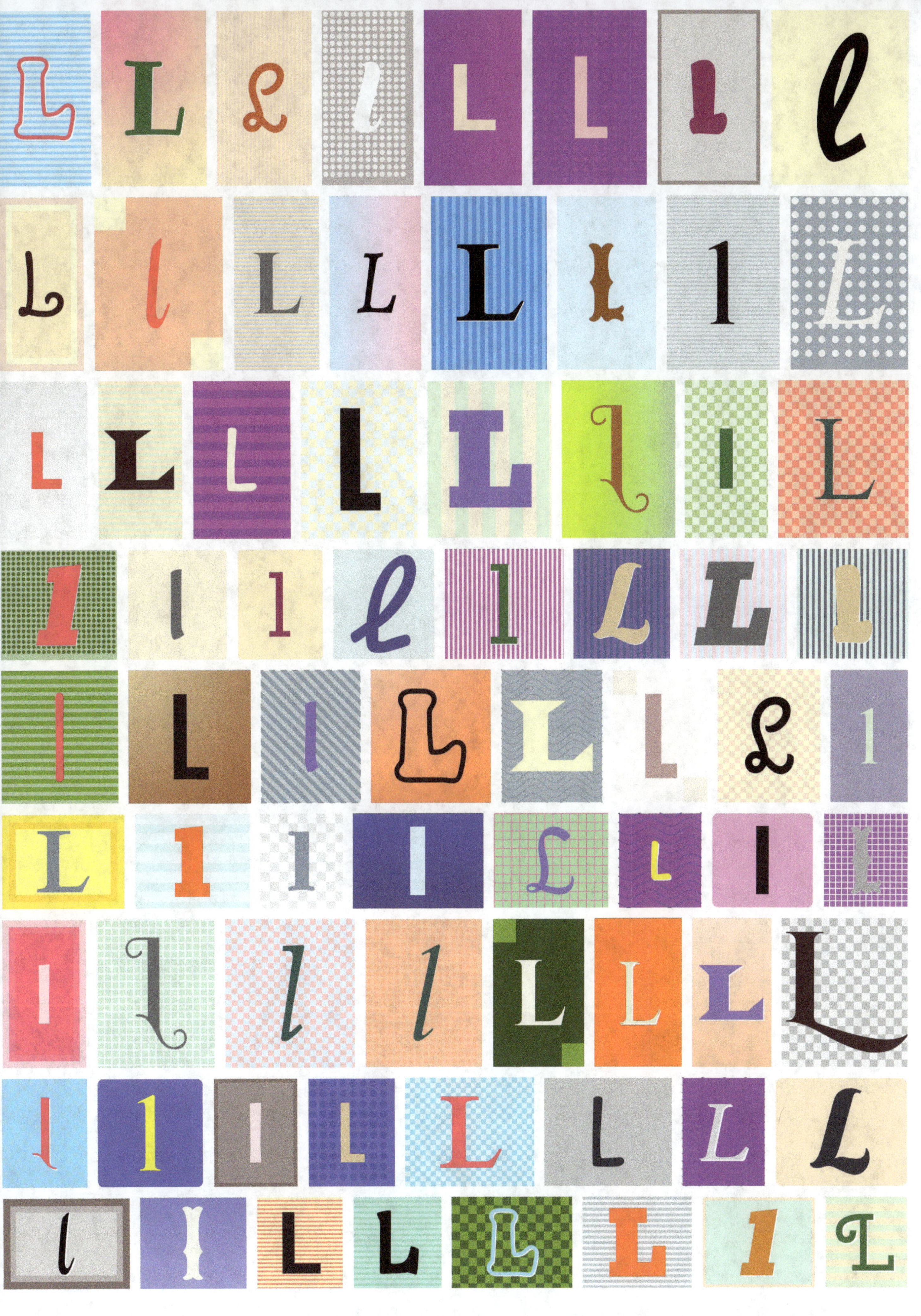

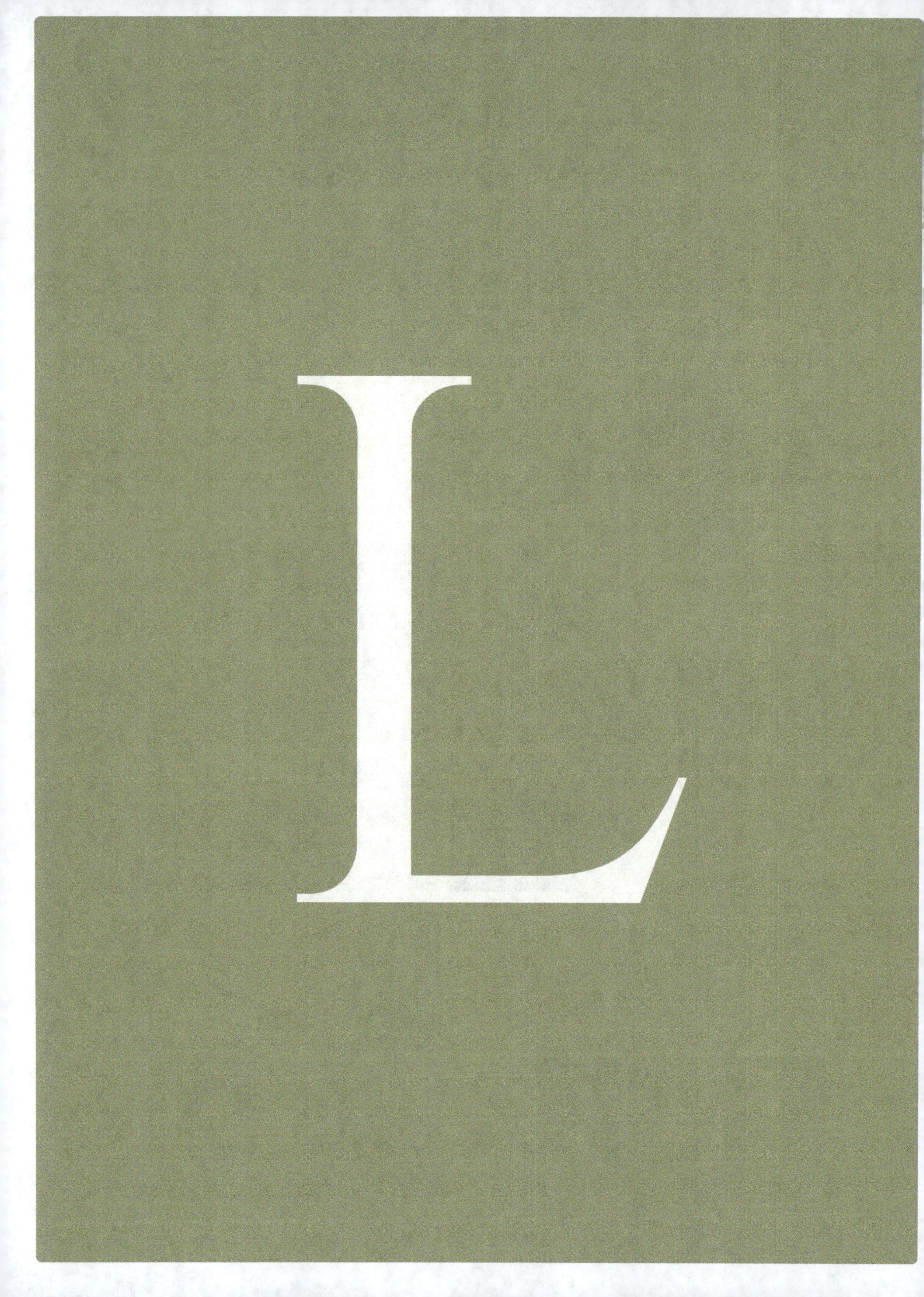

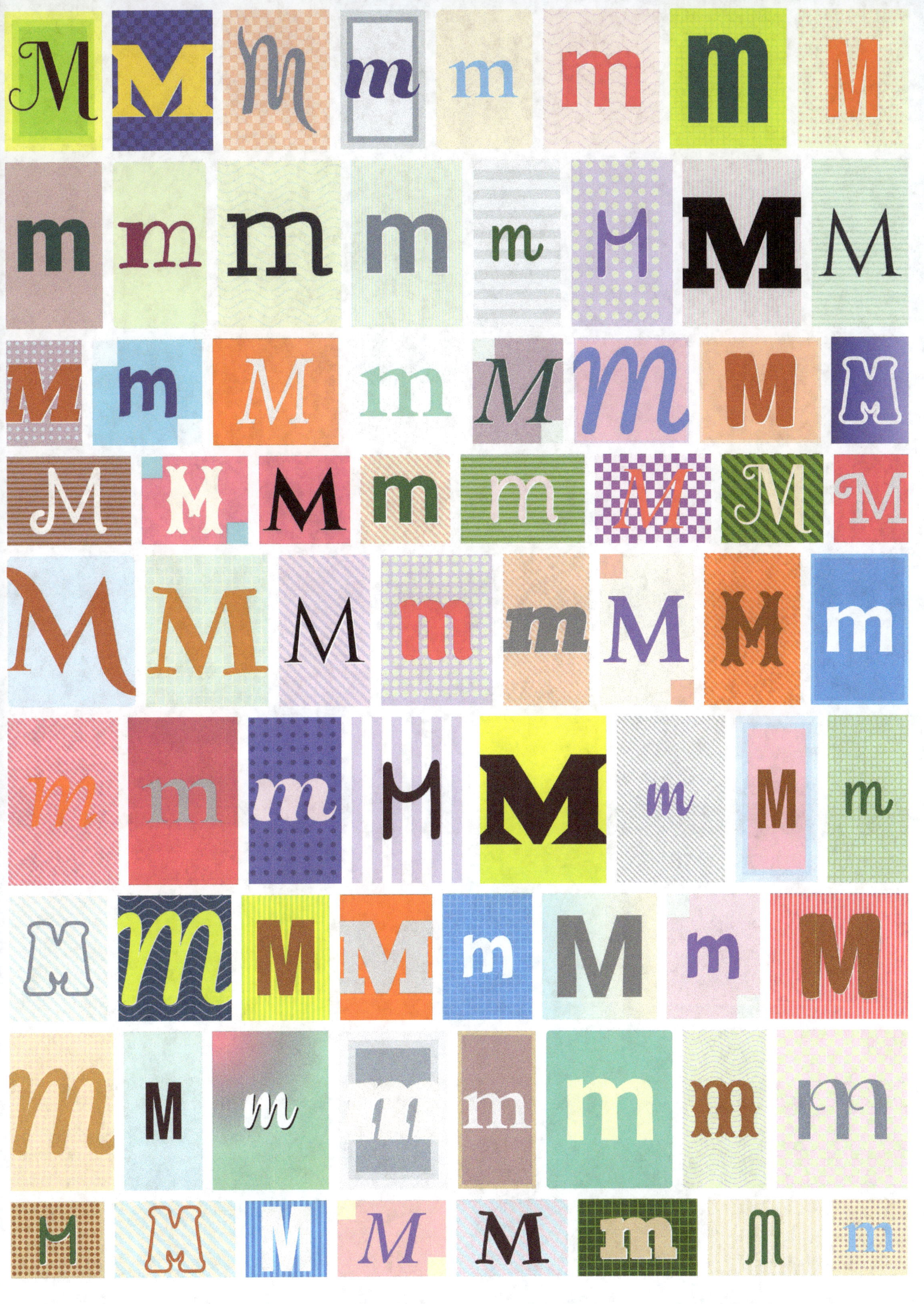

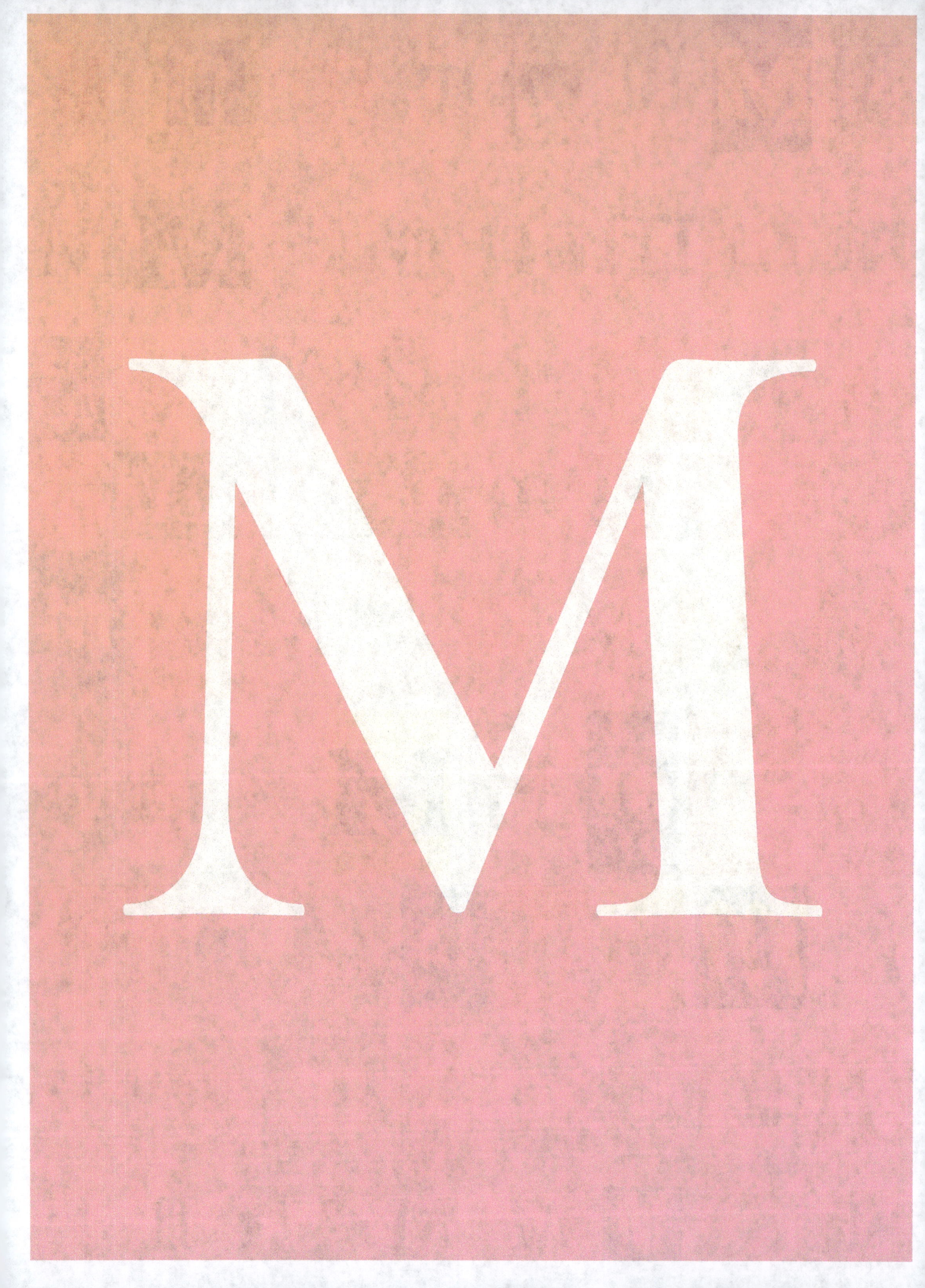

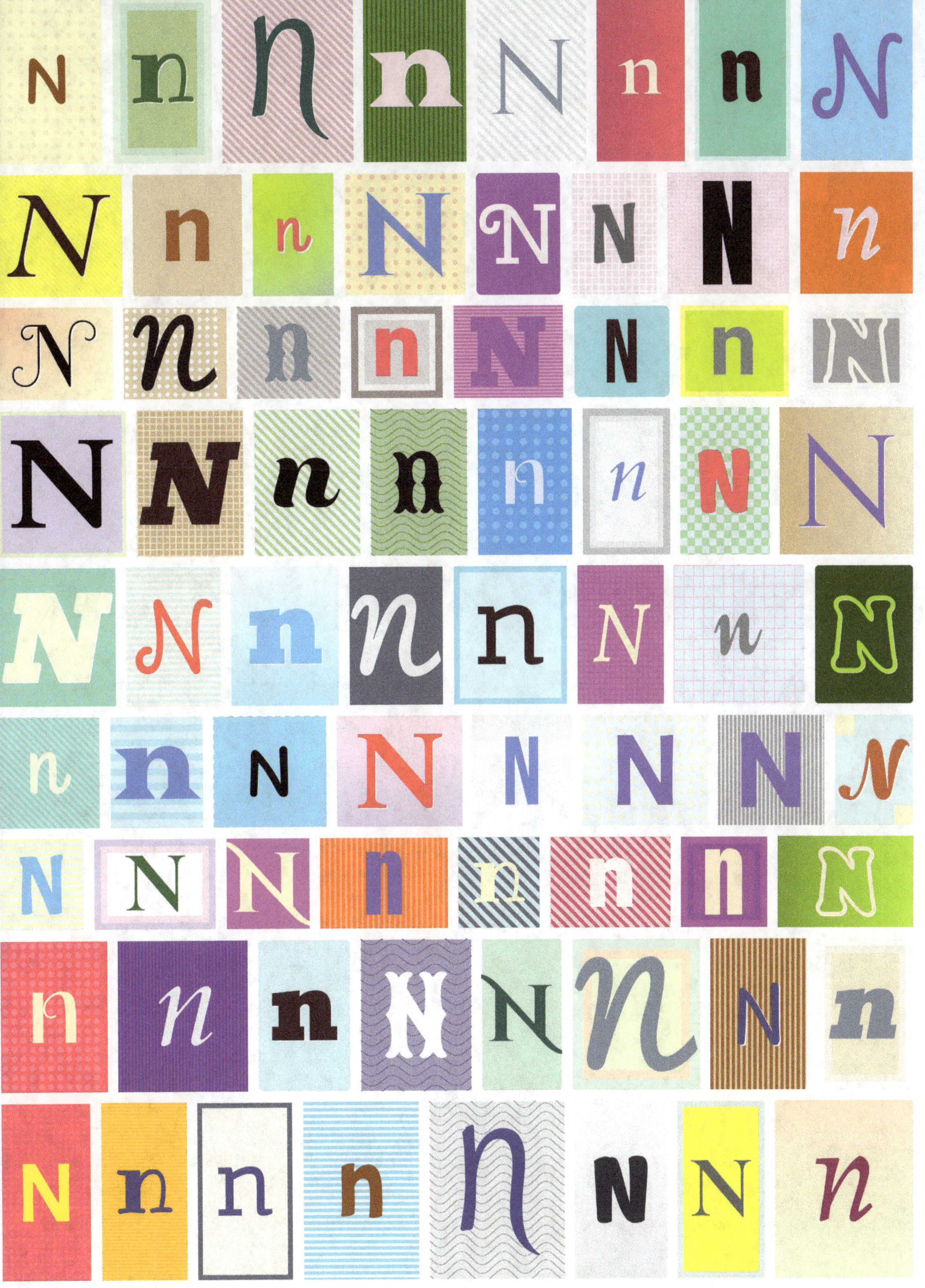

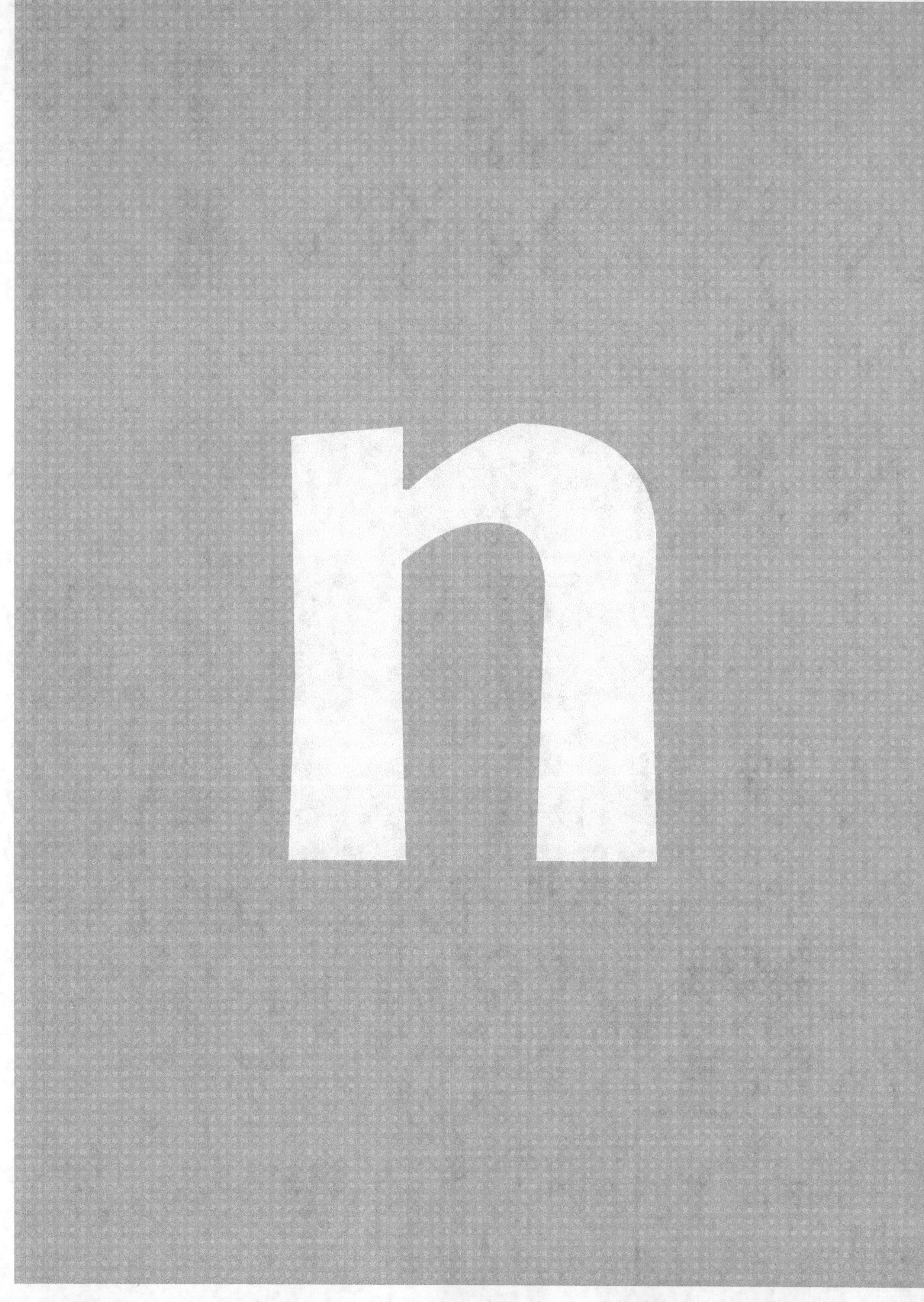

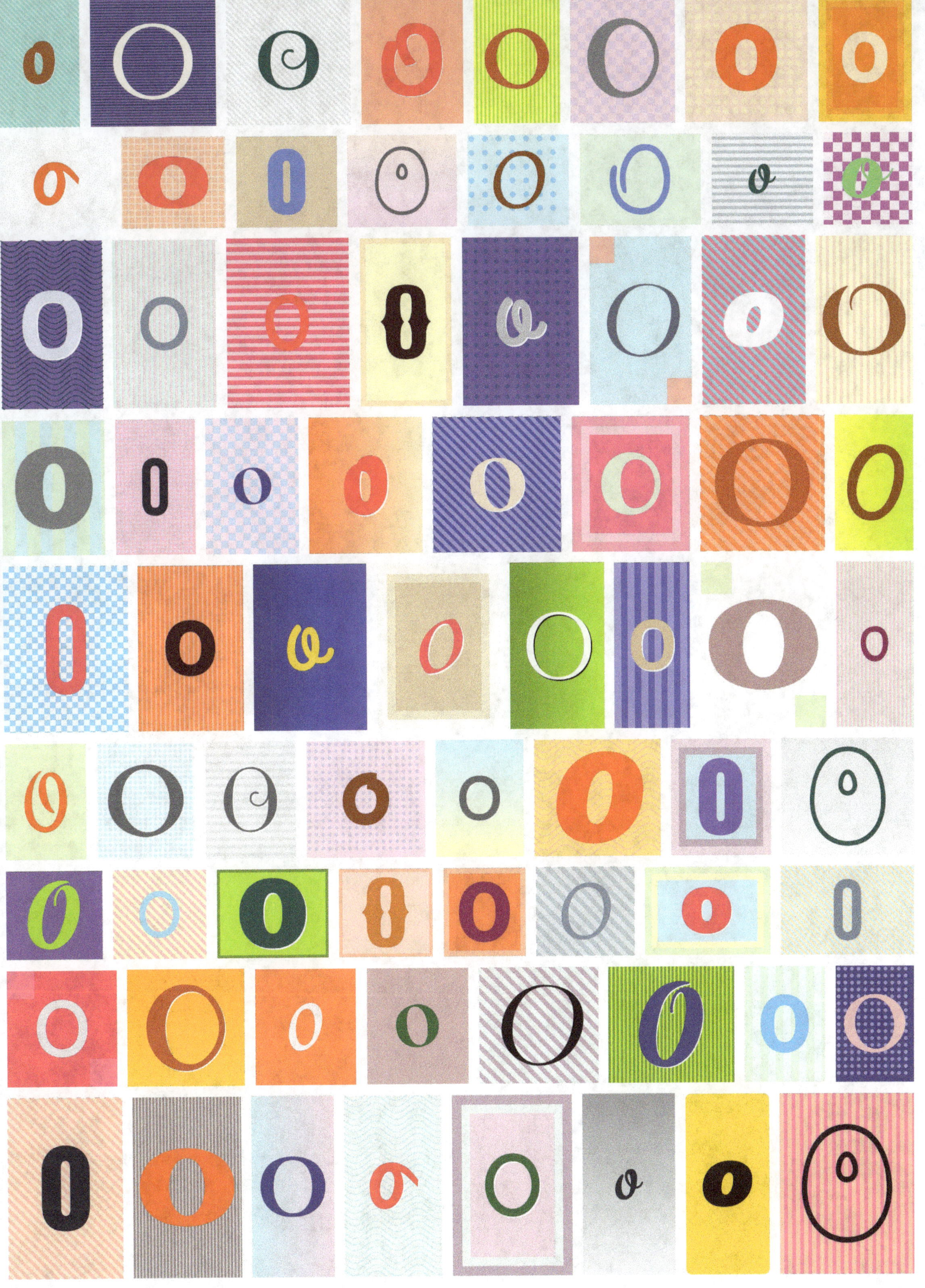

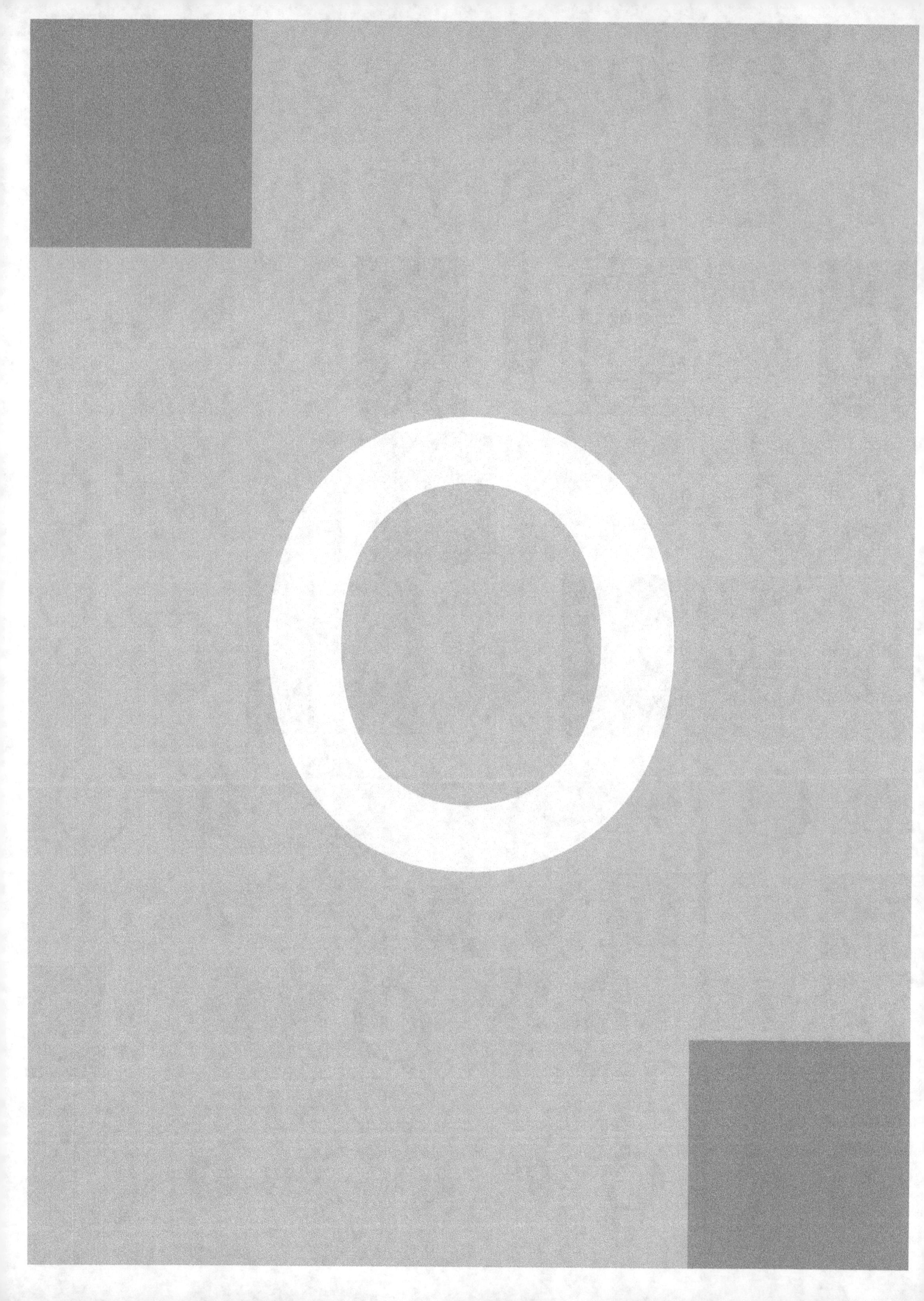

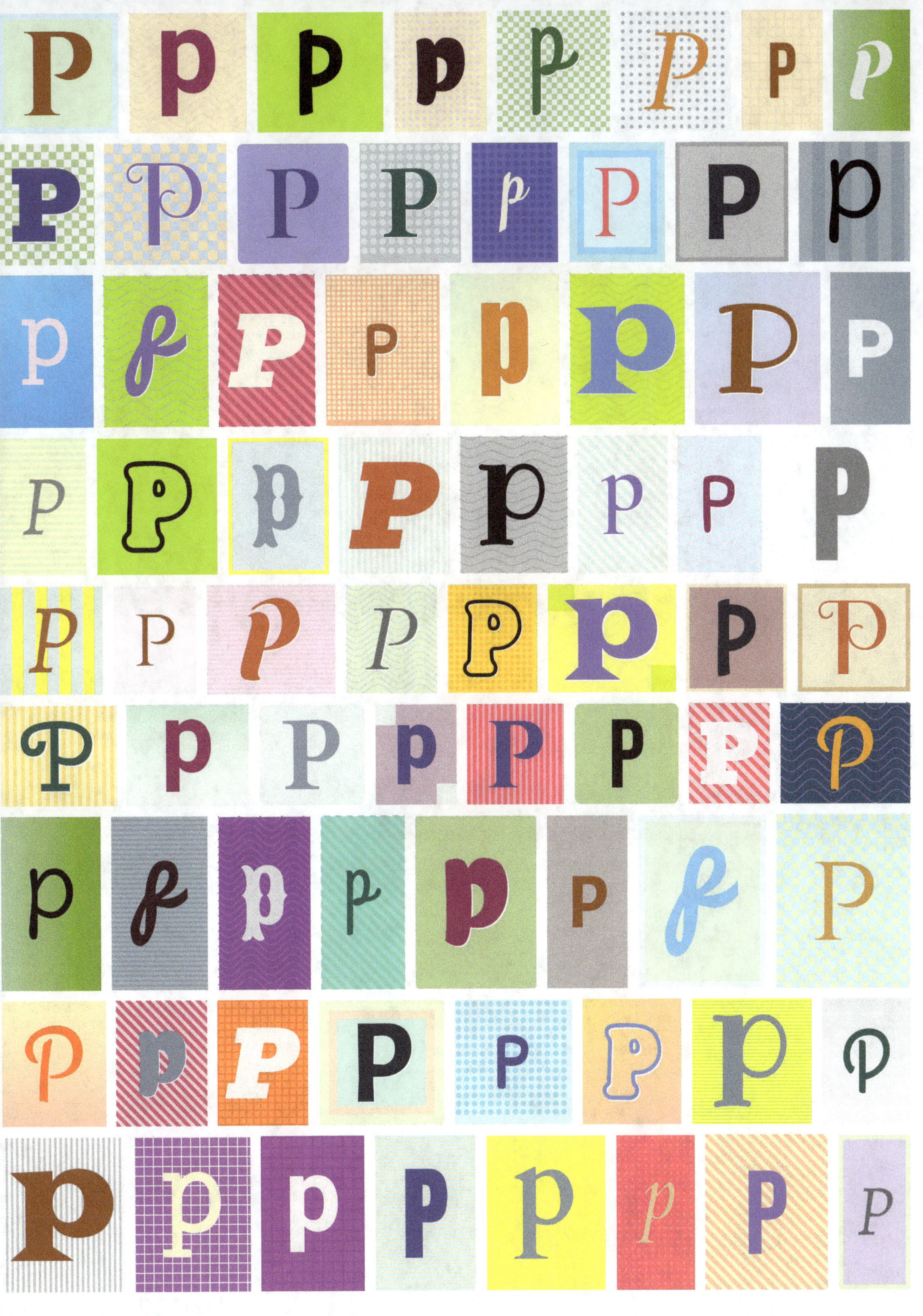

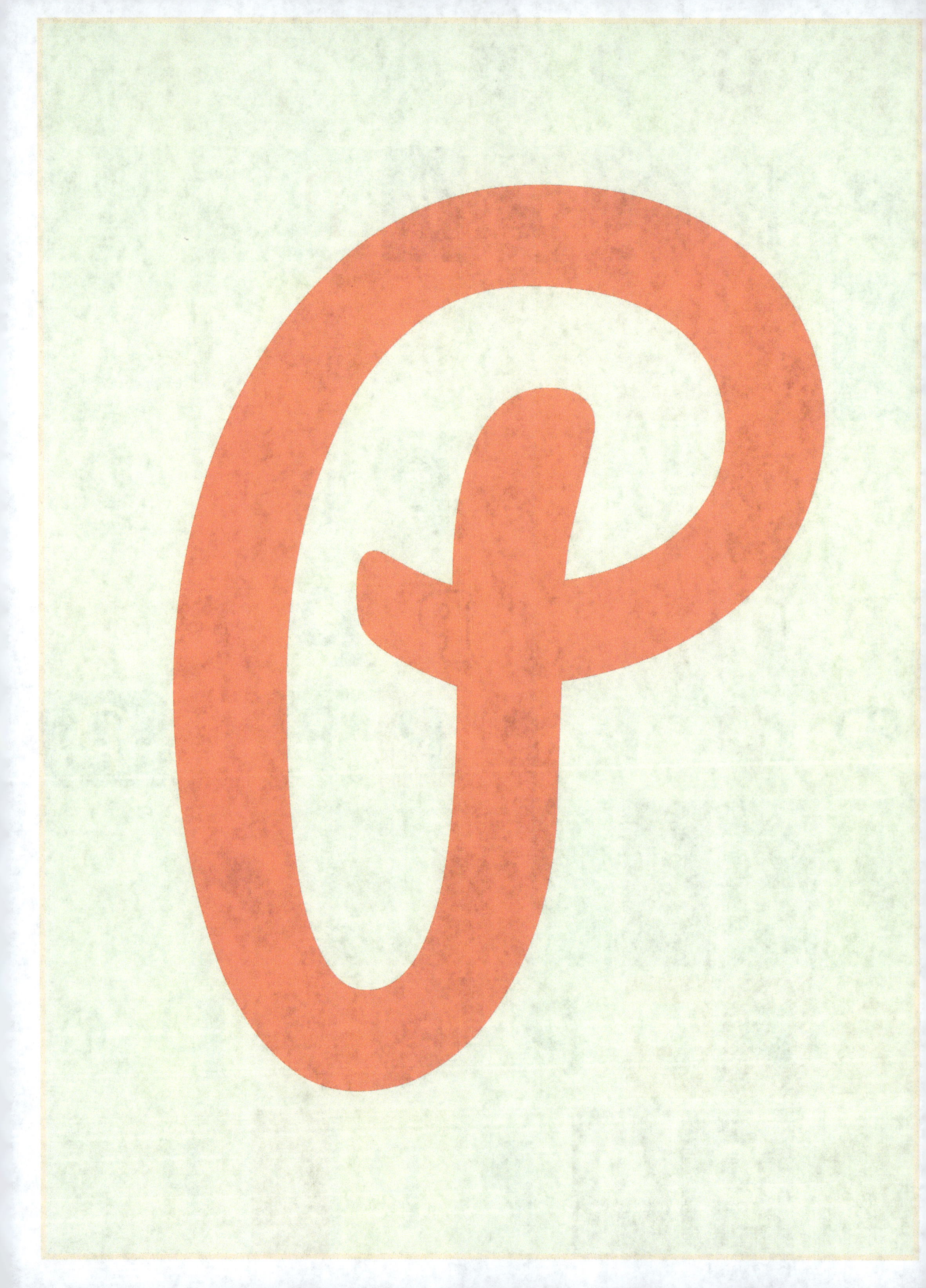

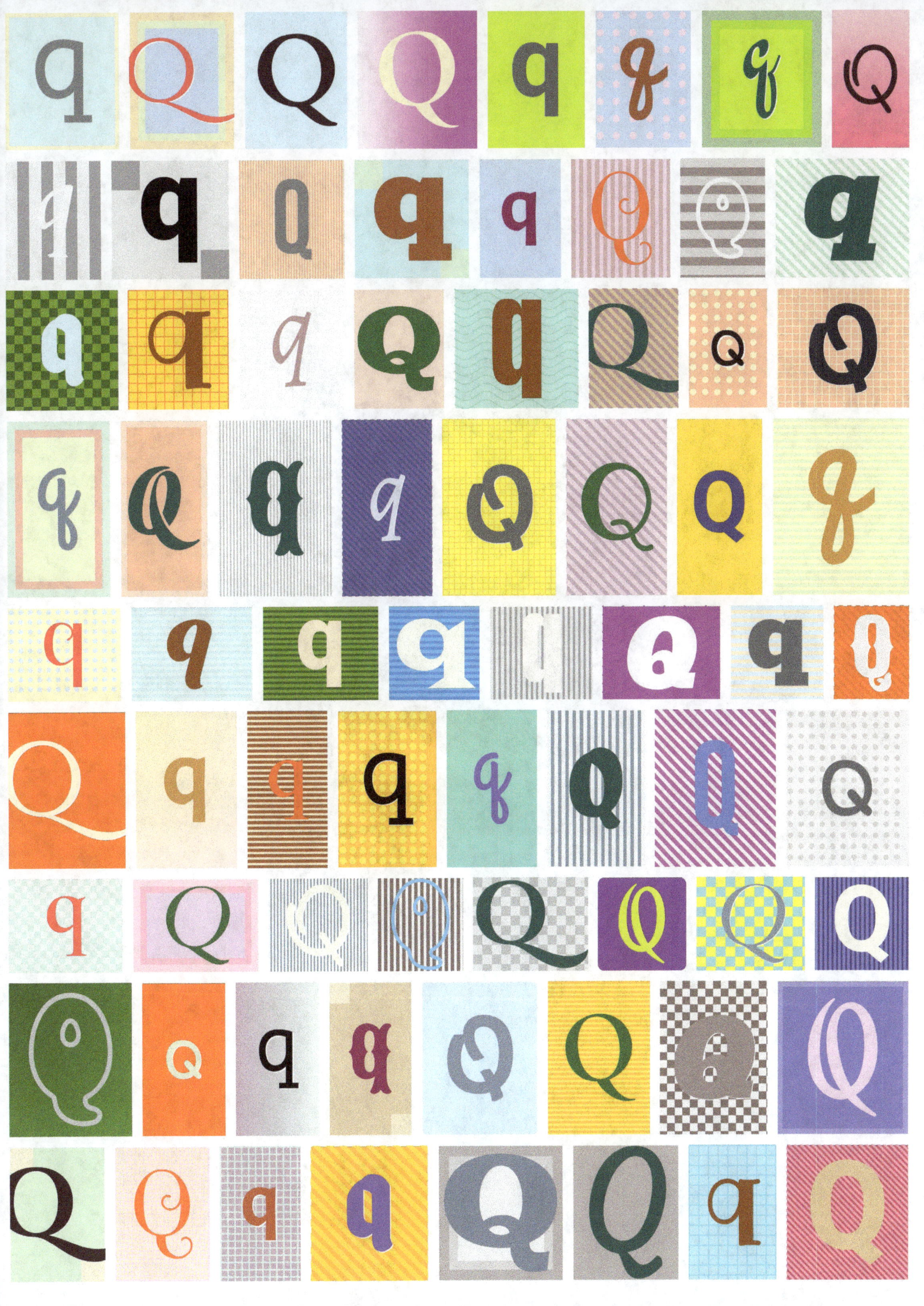

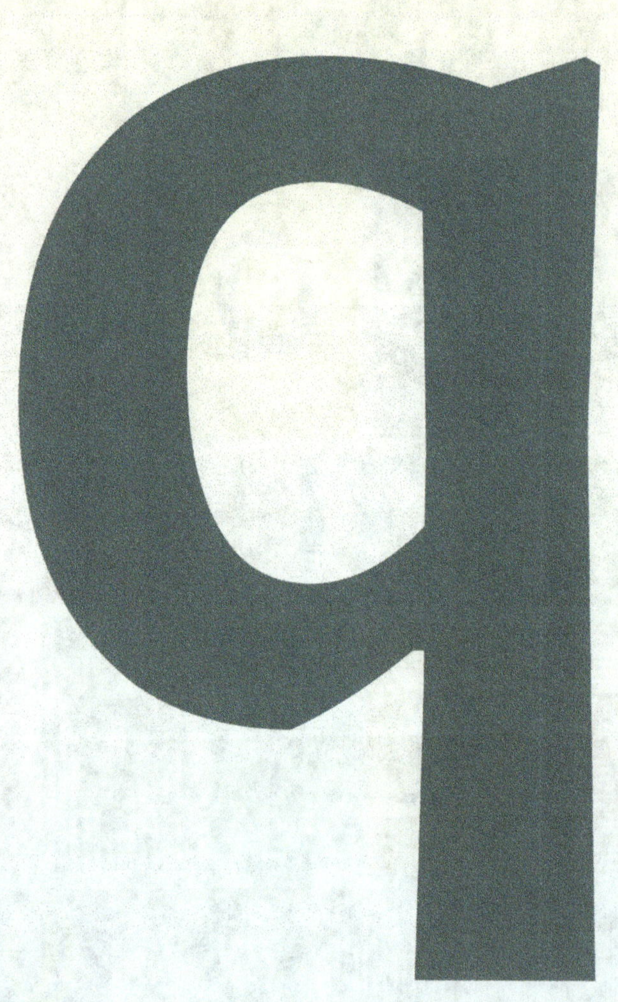

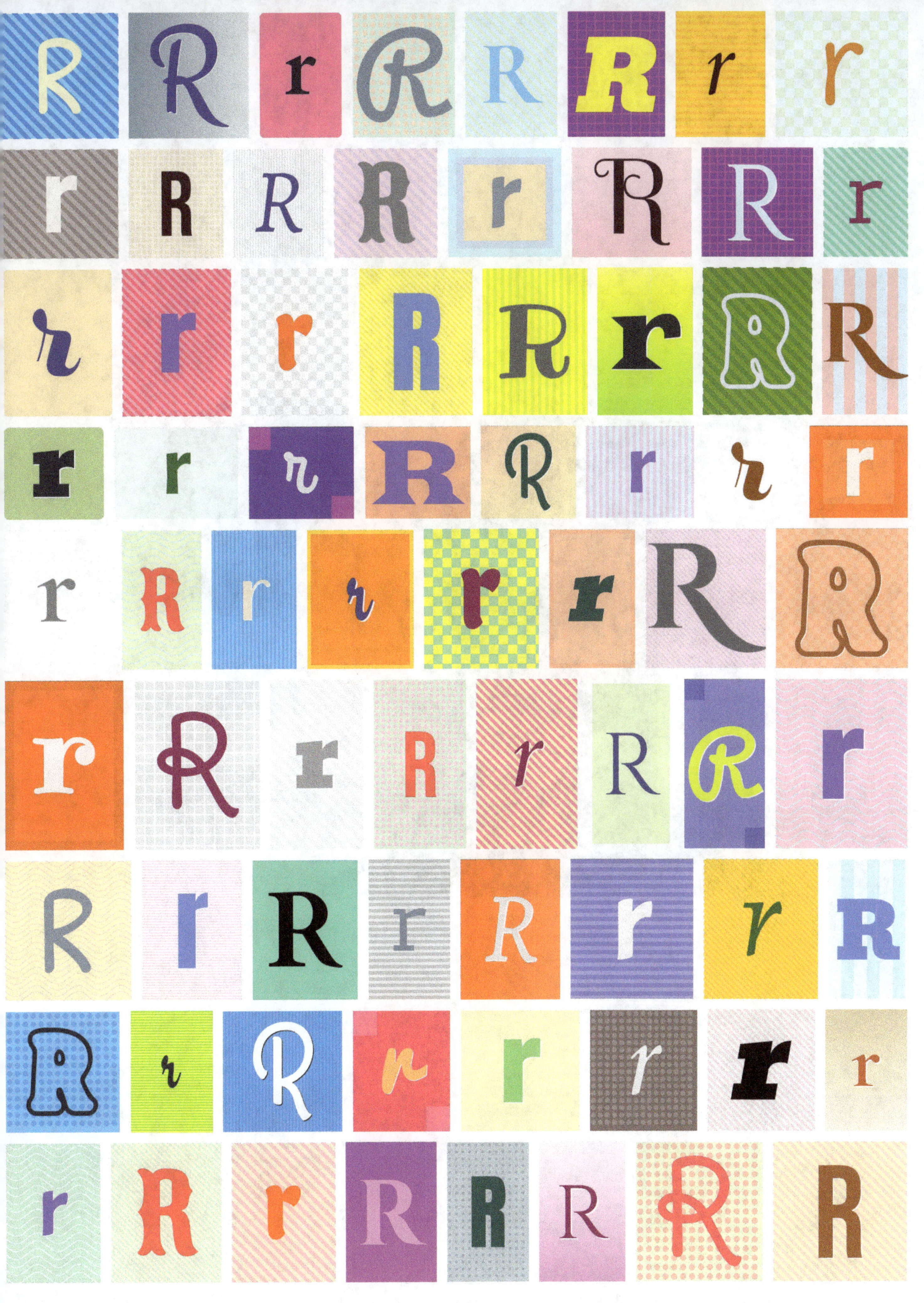

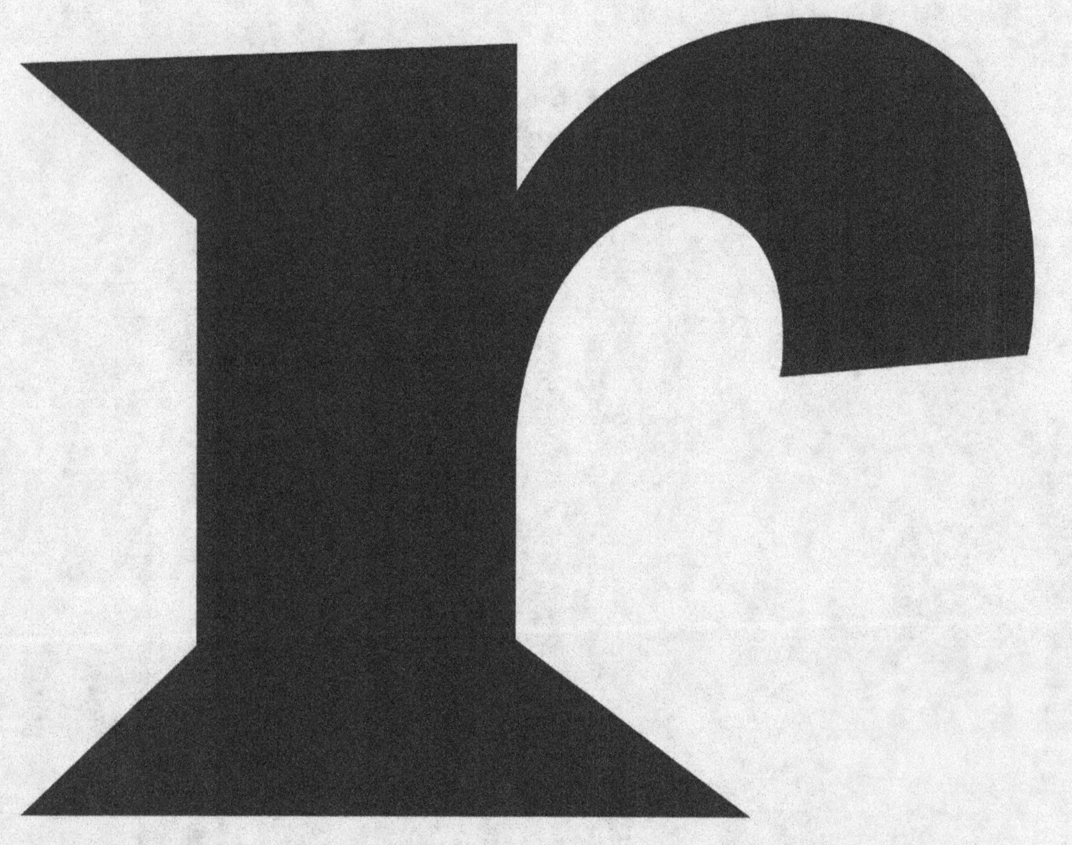

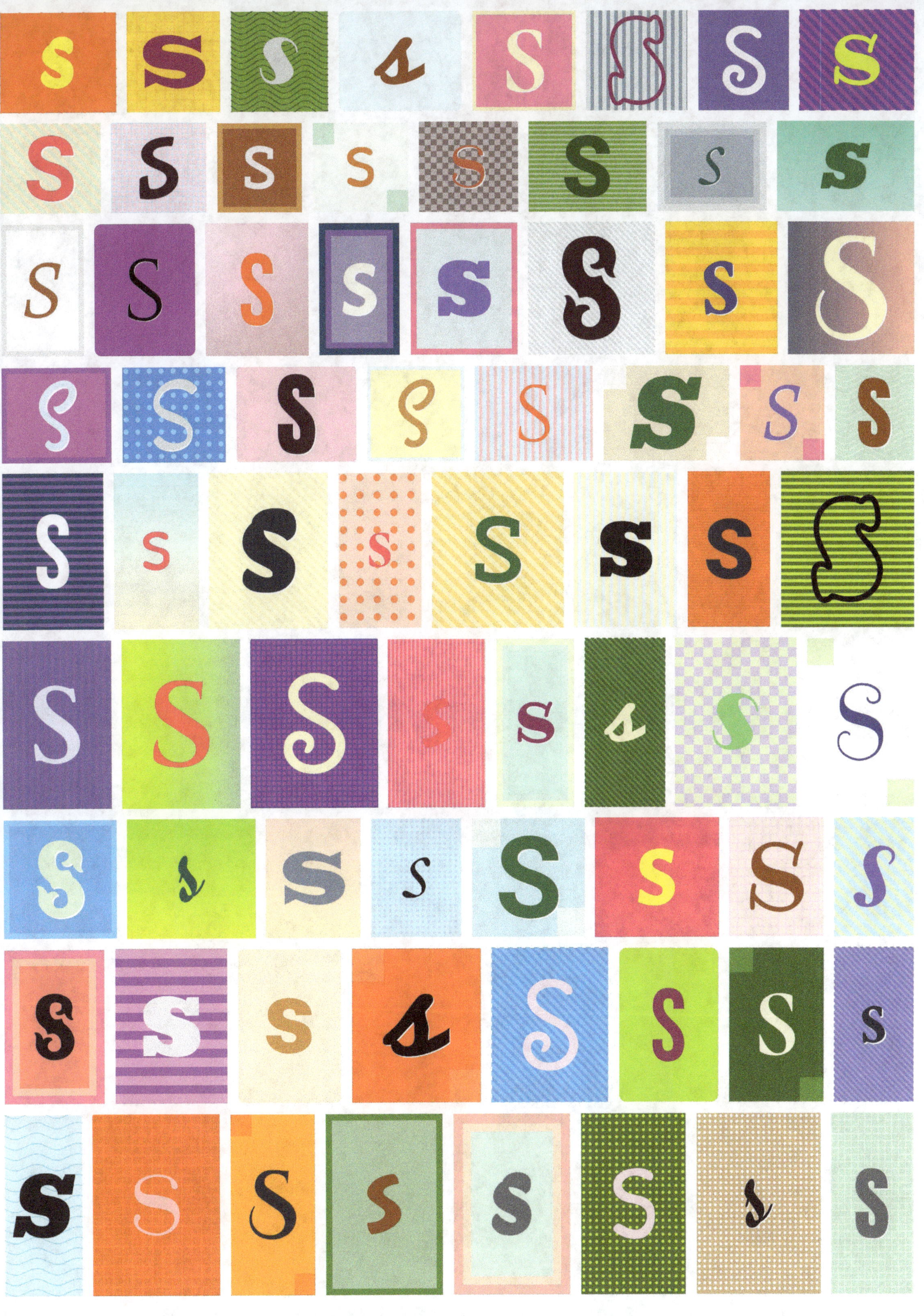

S

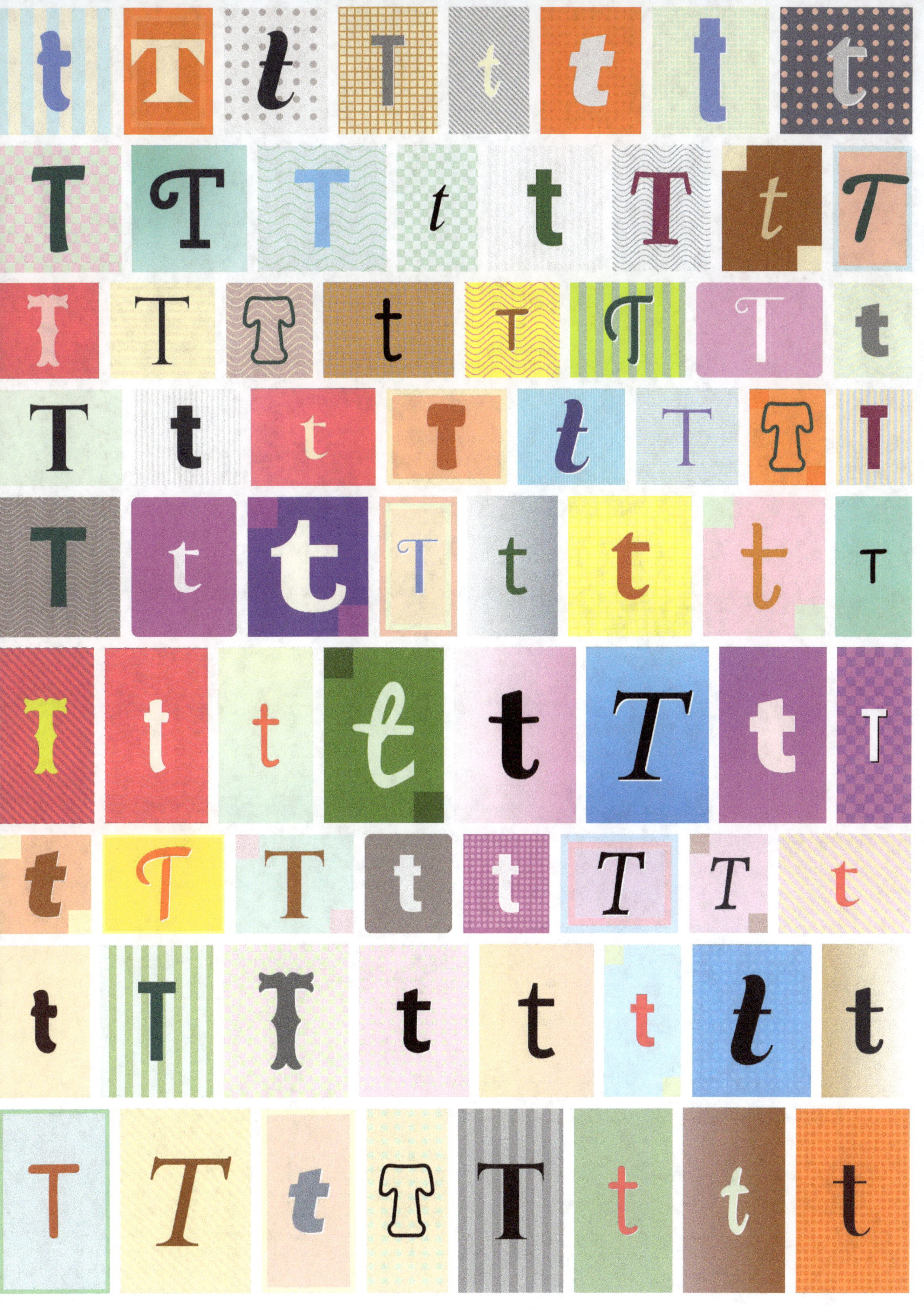

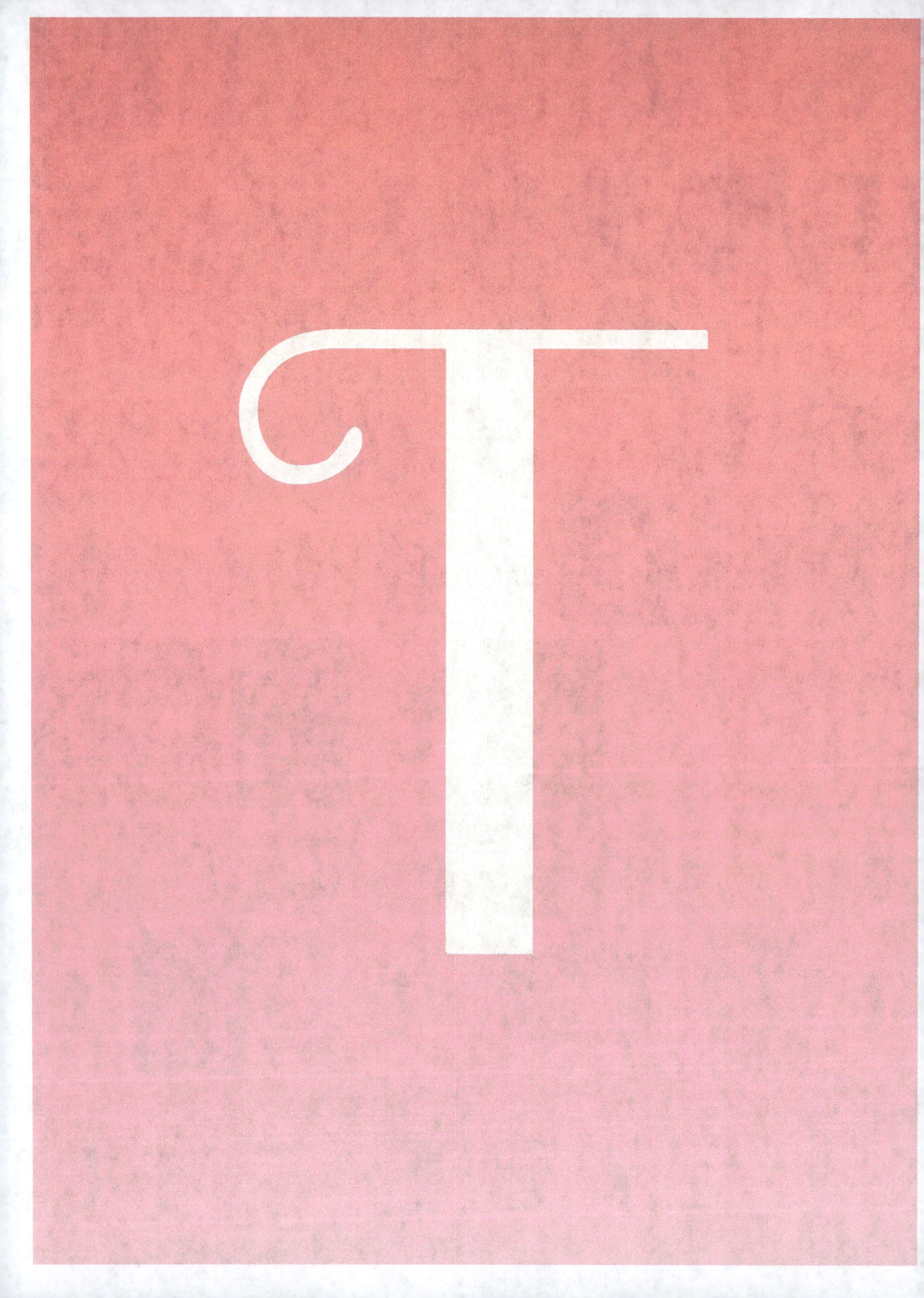

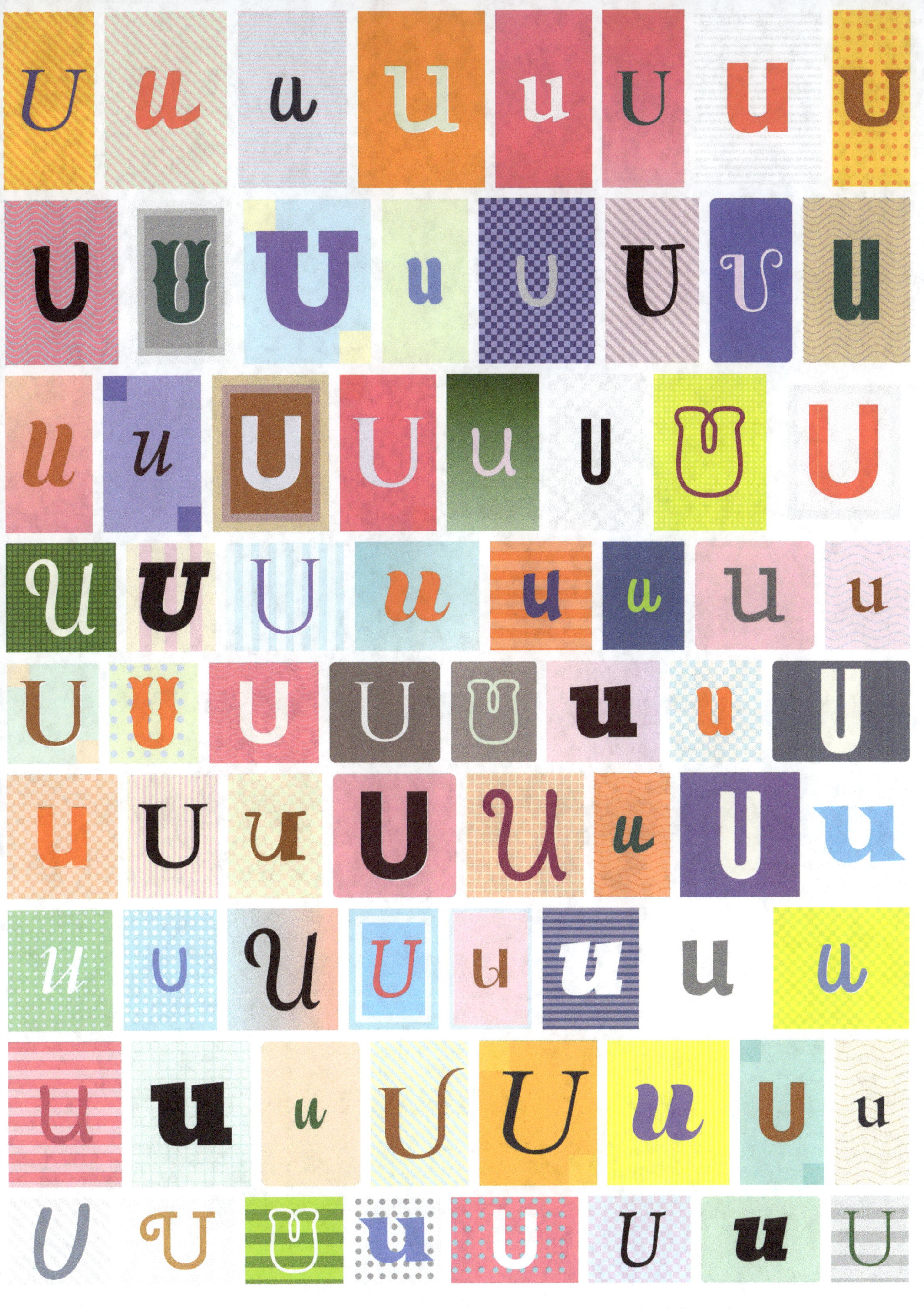

u

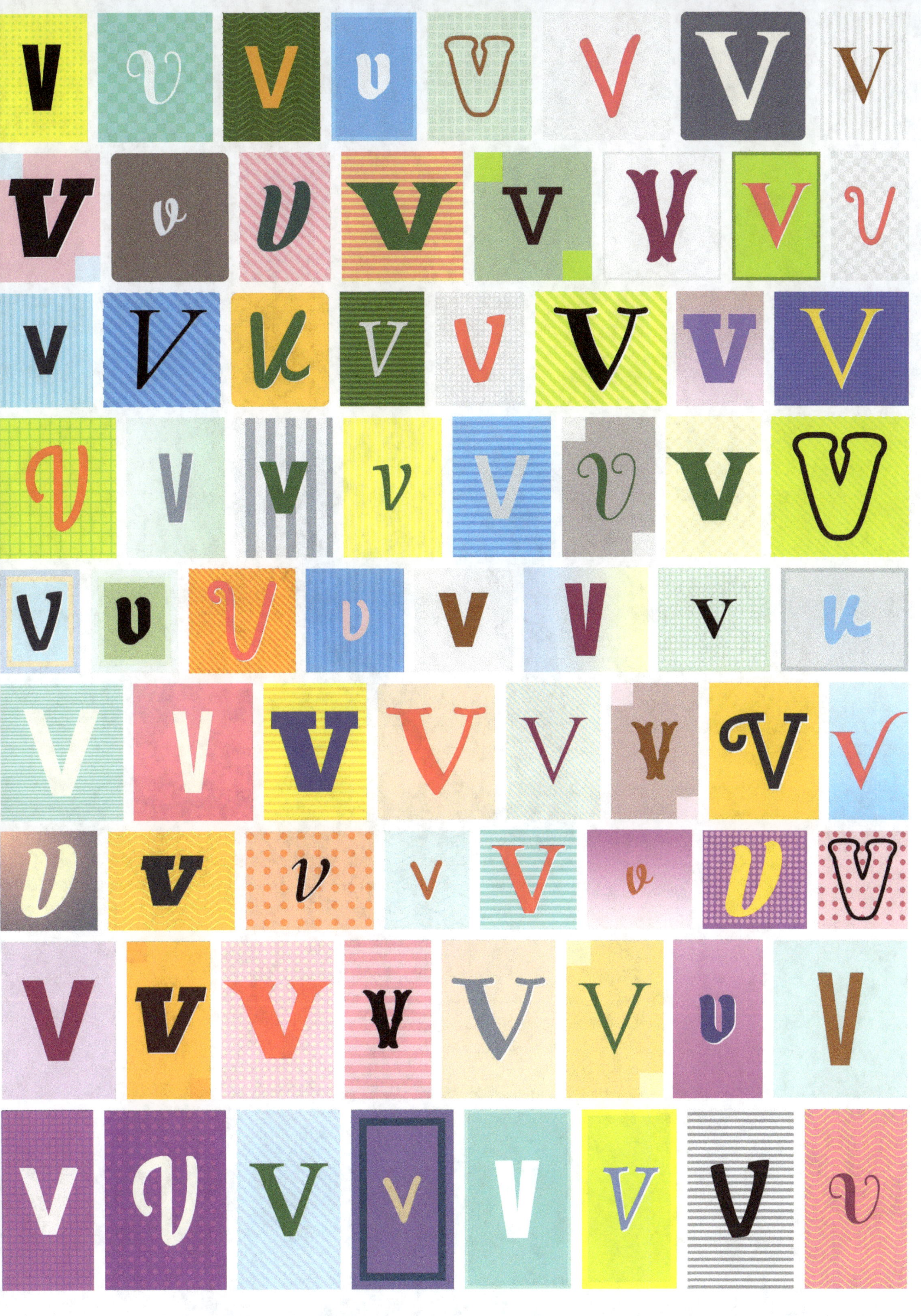

v

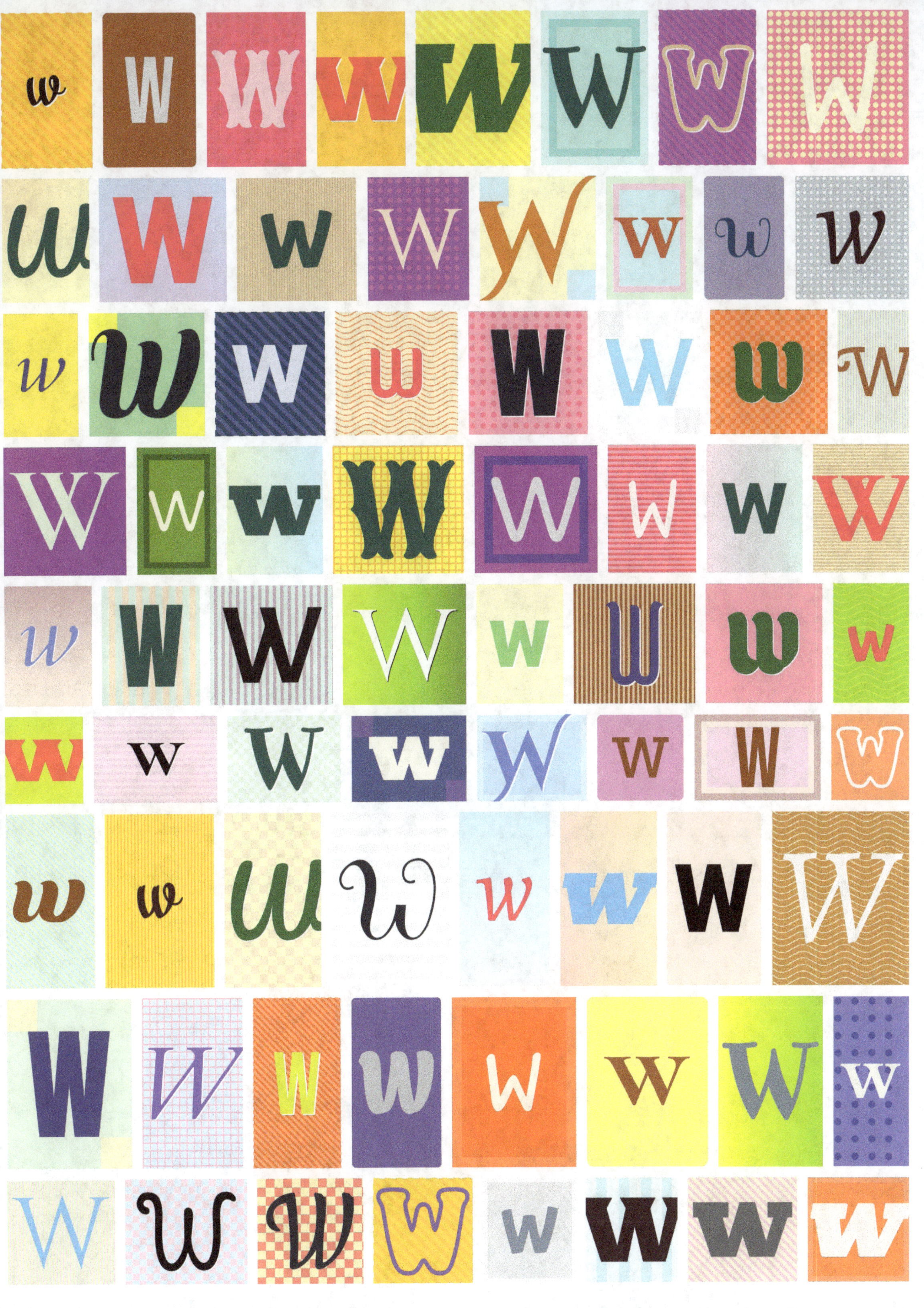

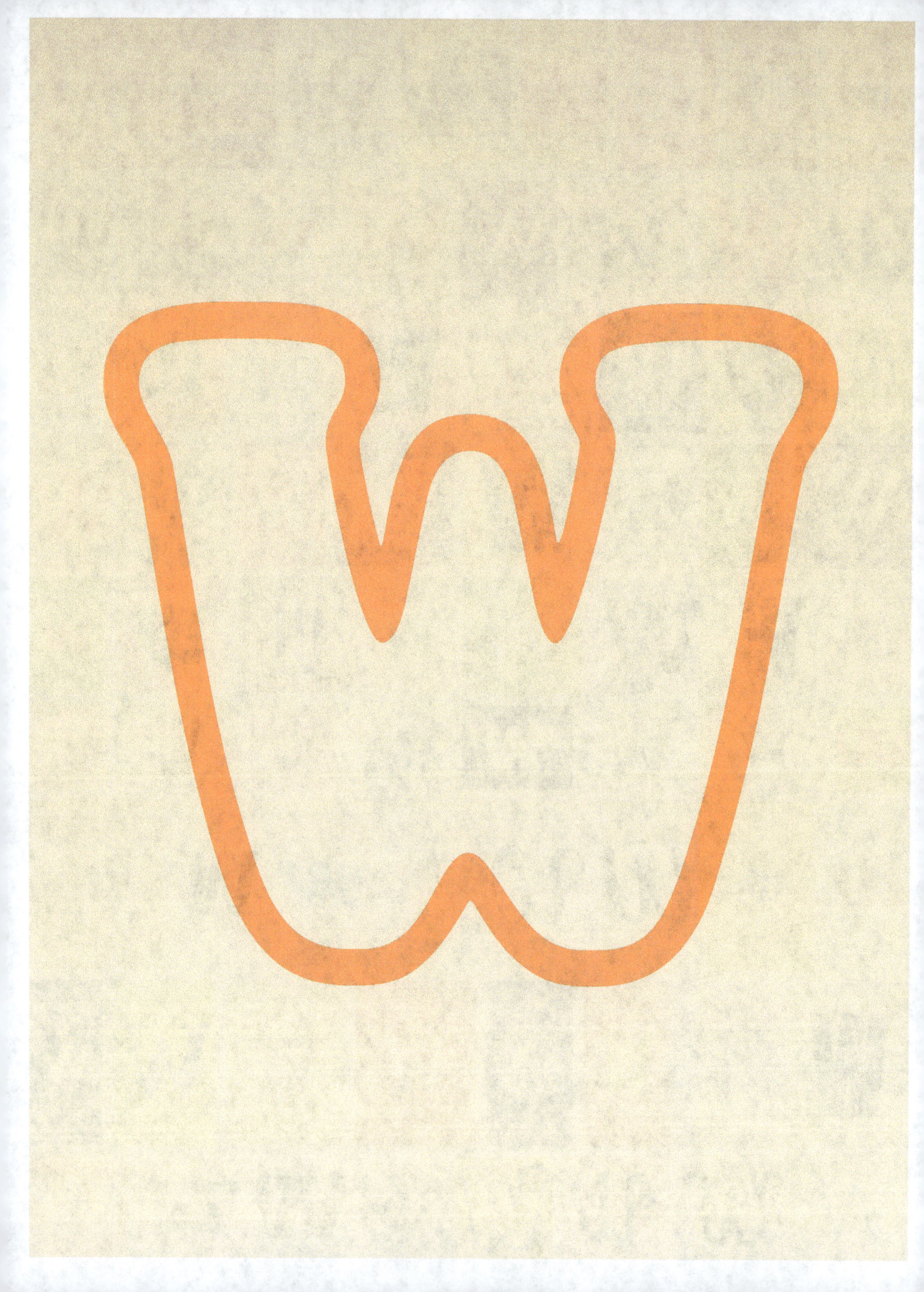

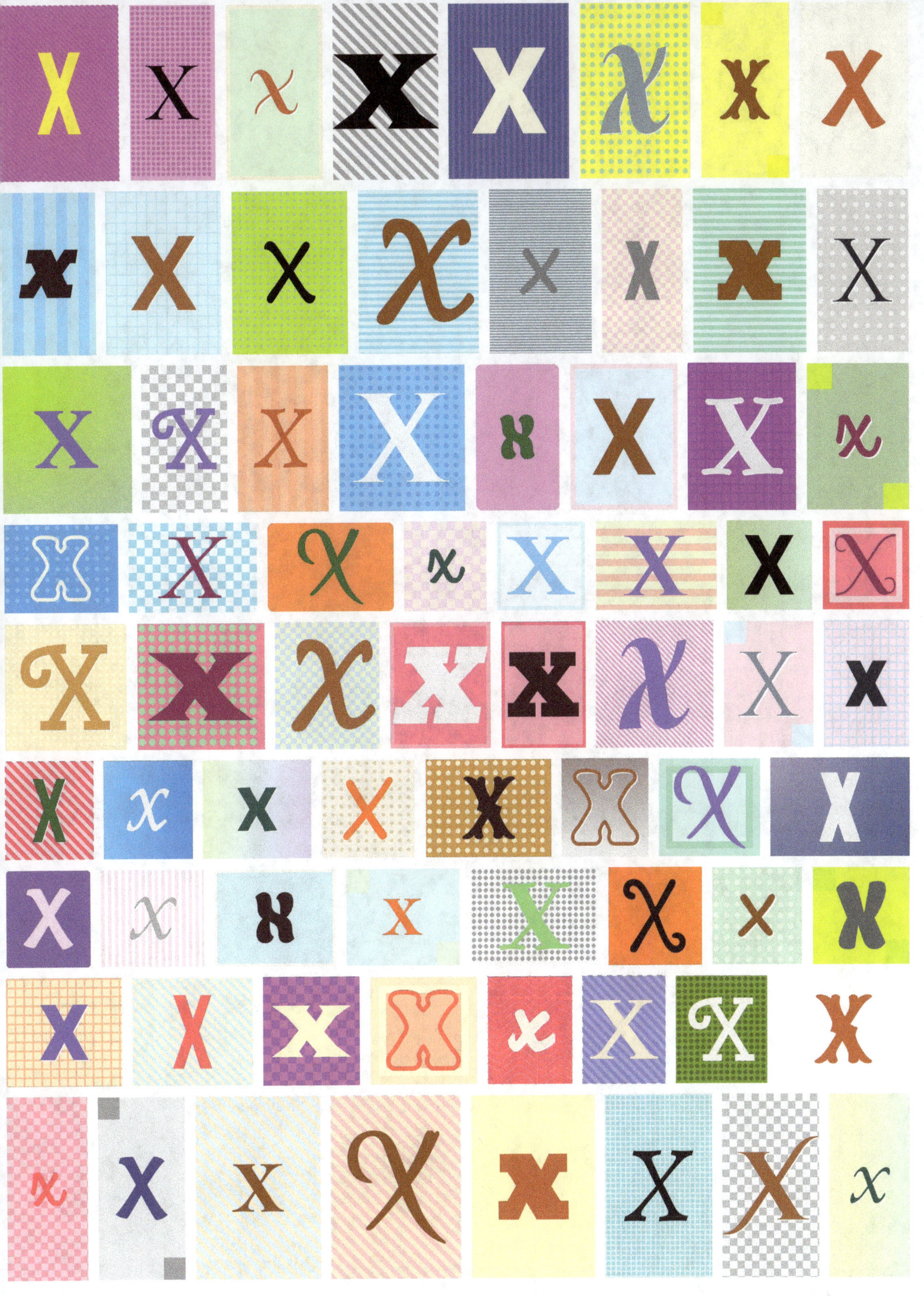

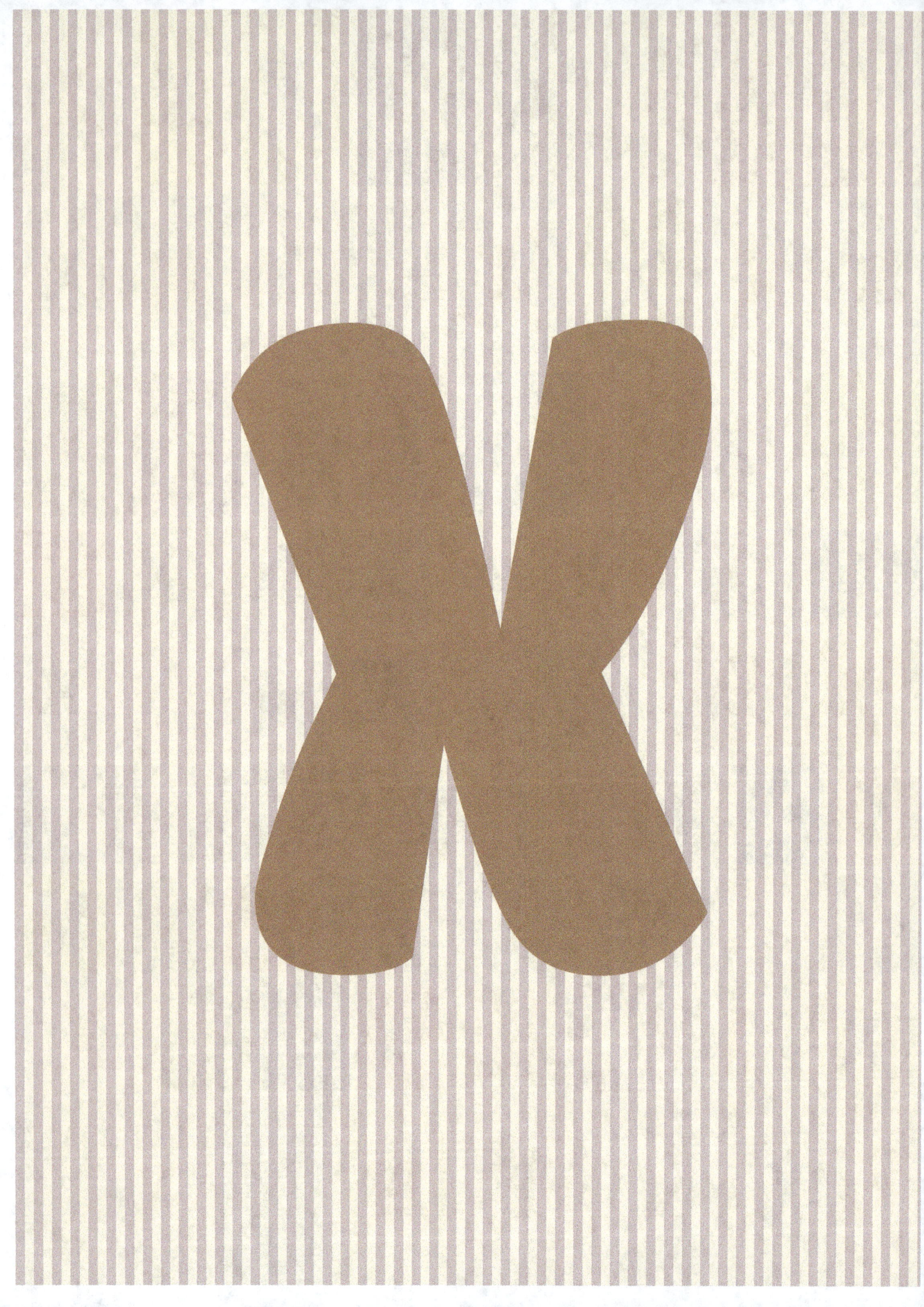

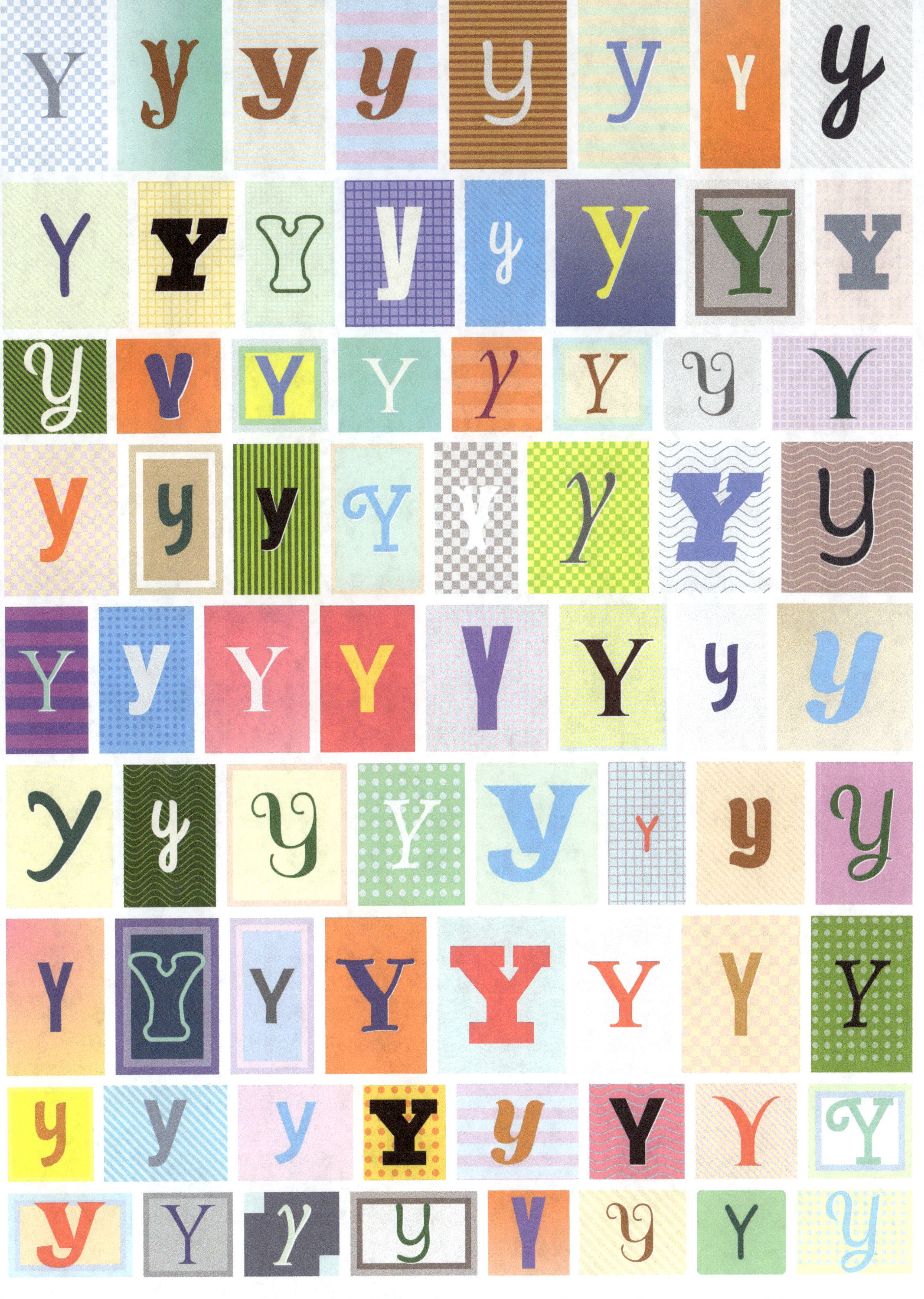

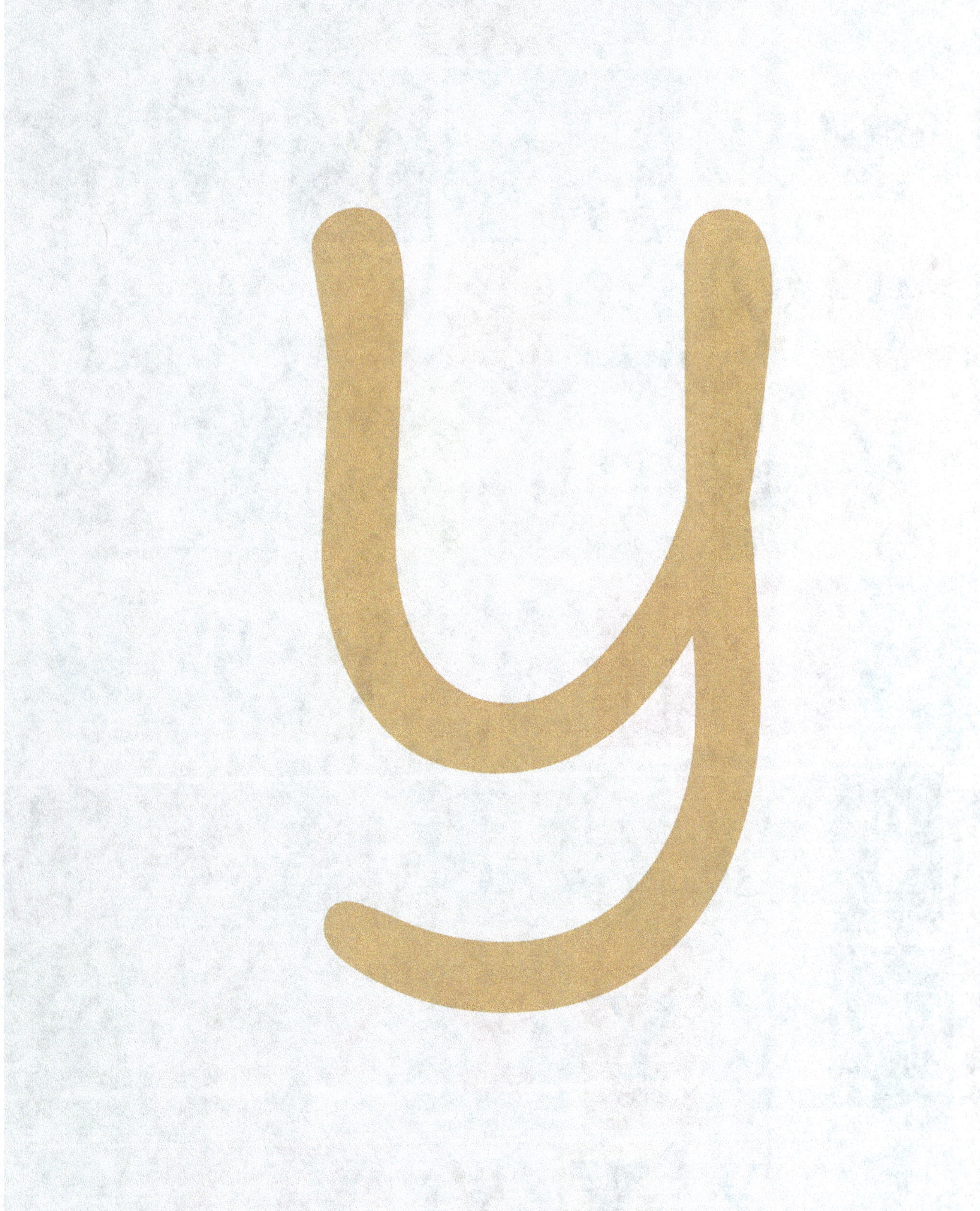

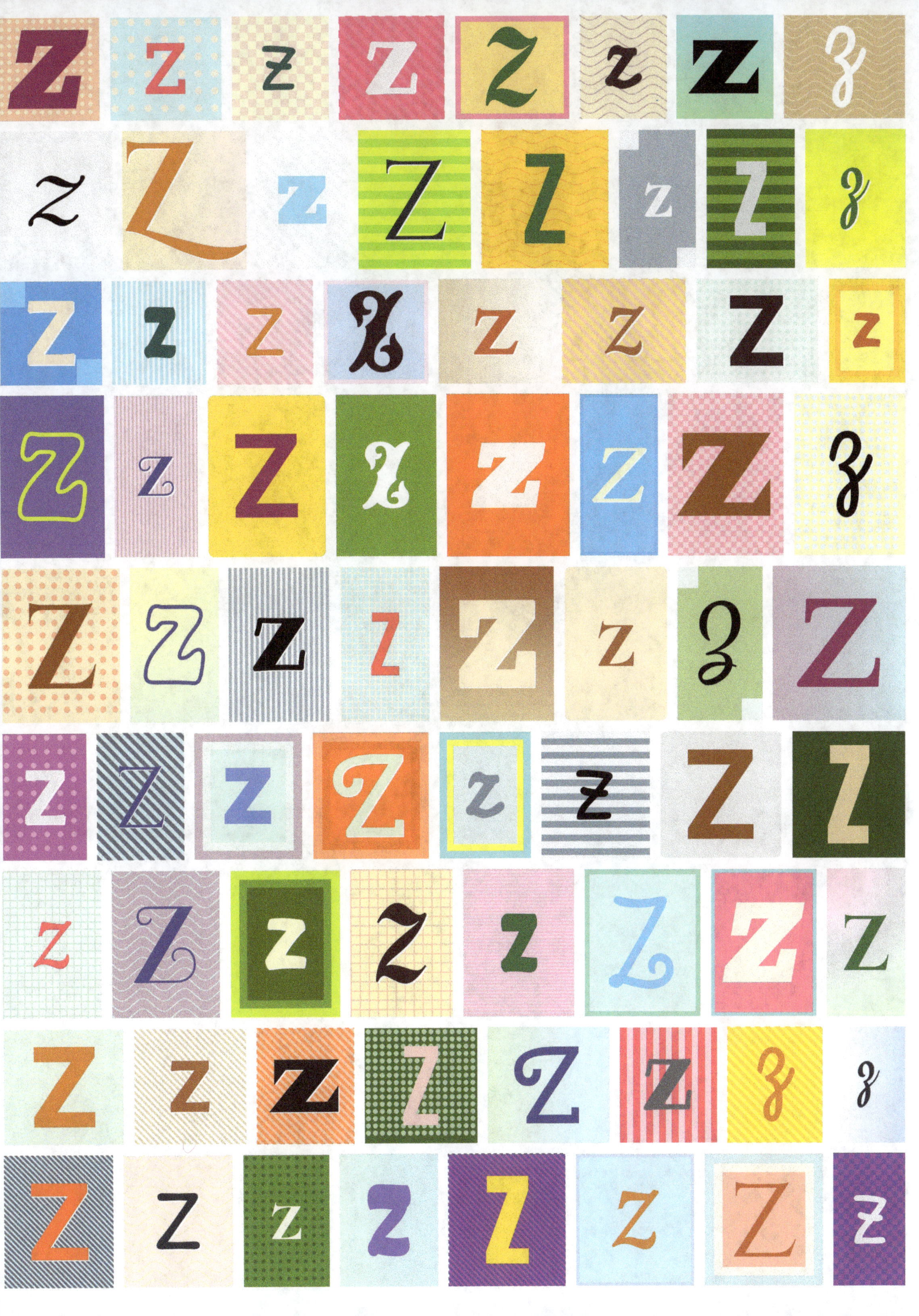

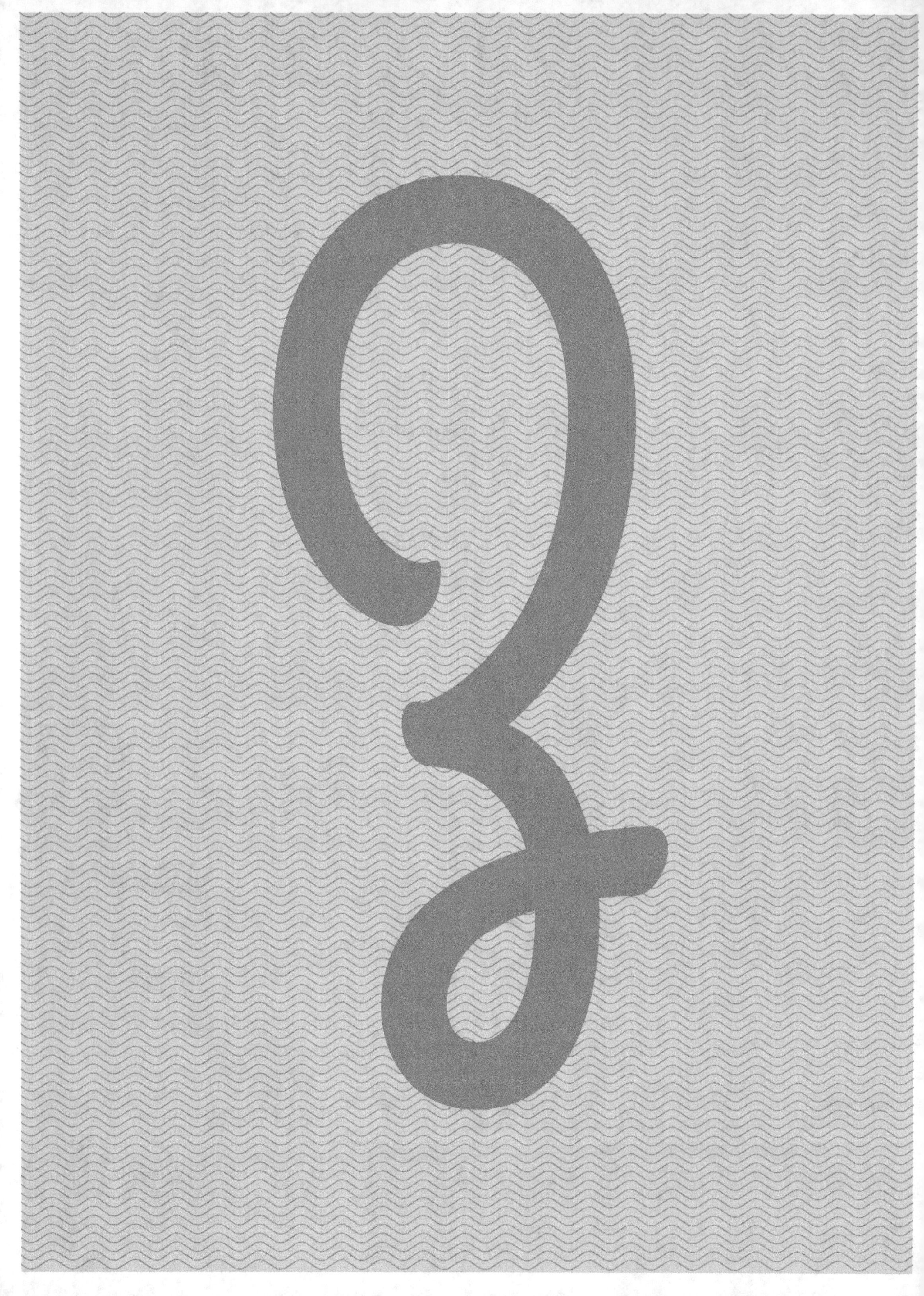

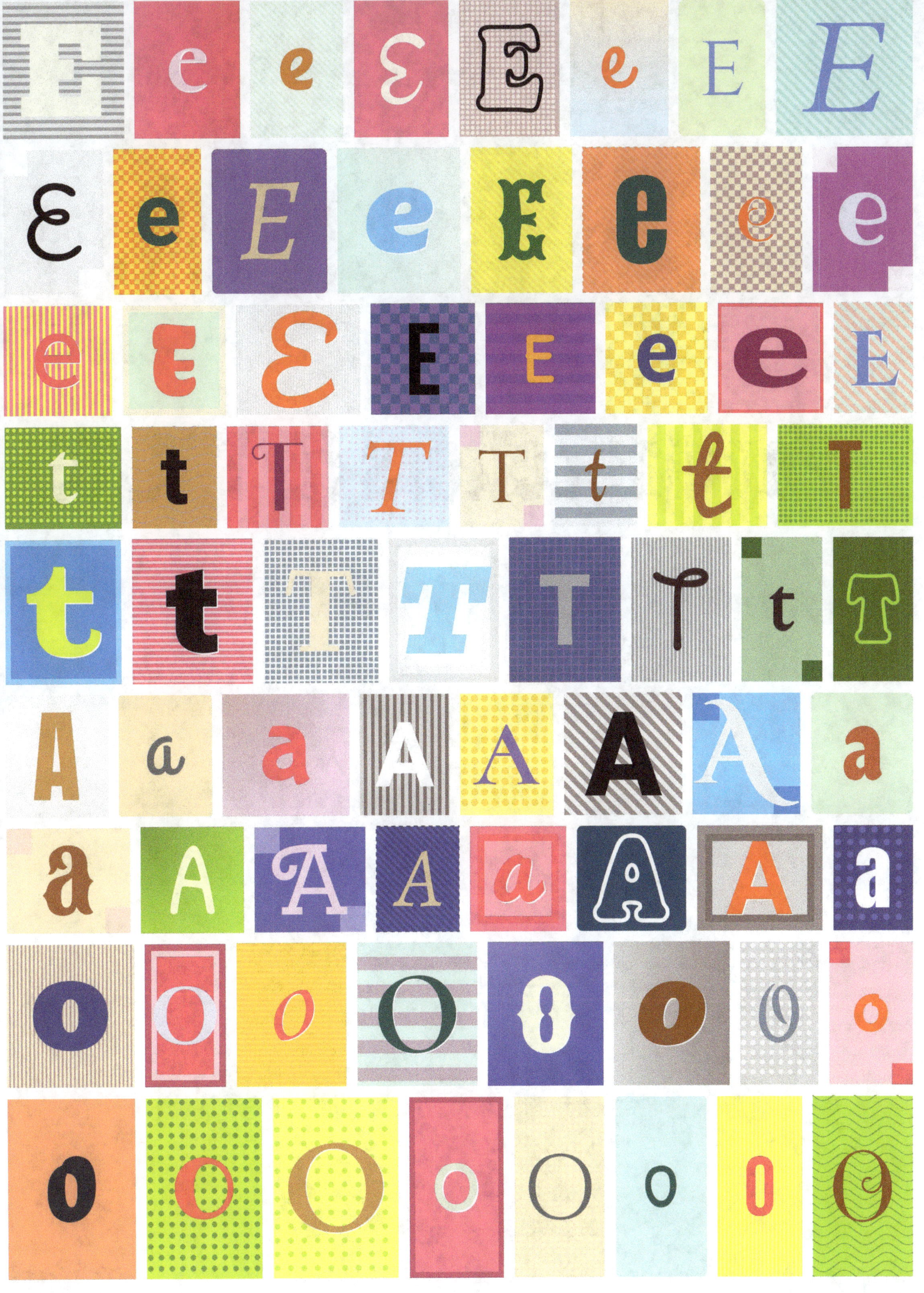

Popular Letters (E, T, A, O)

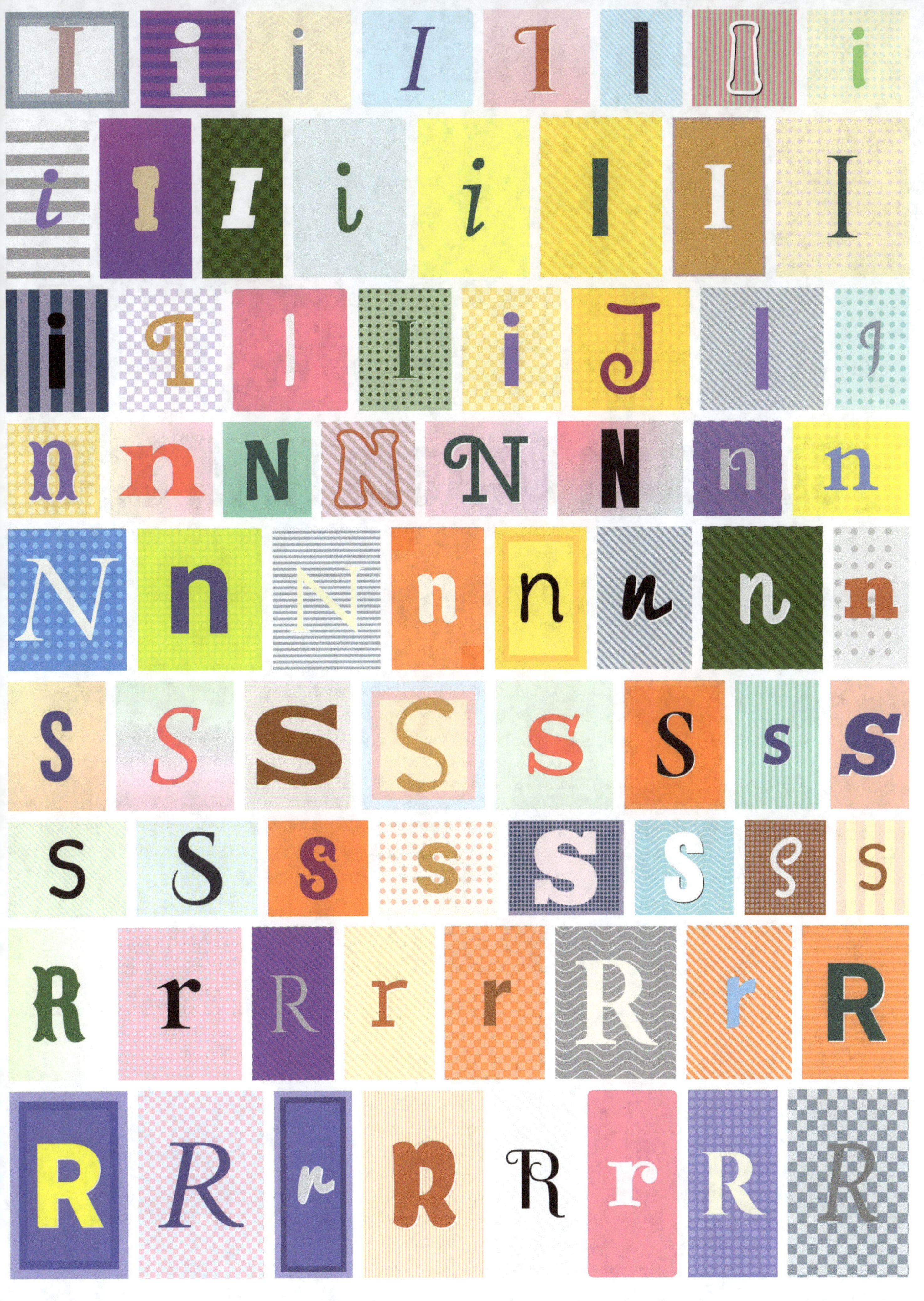

Common Letters (I, N, S, R)

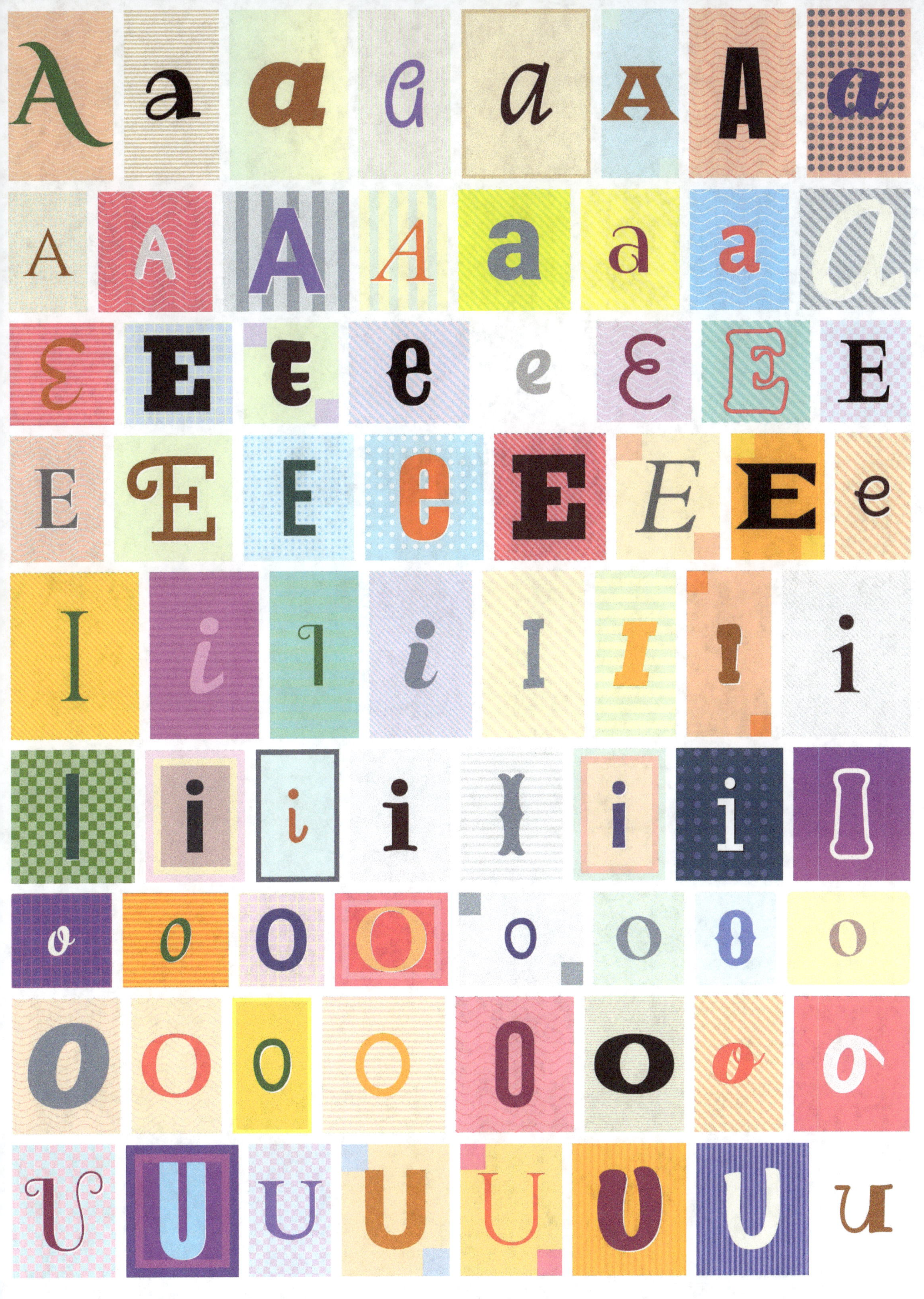

All Vowels

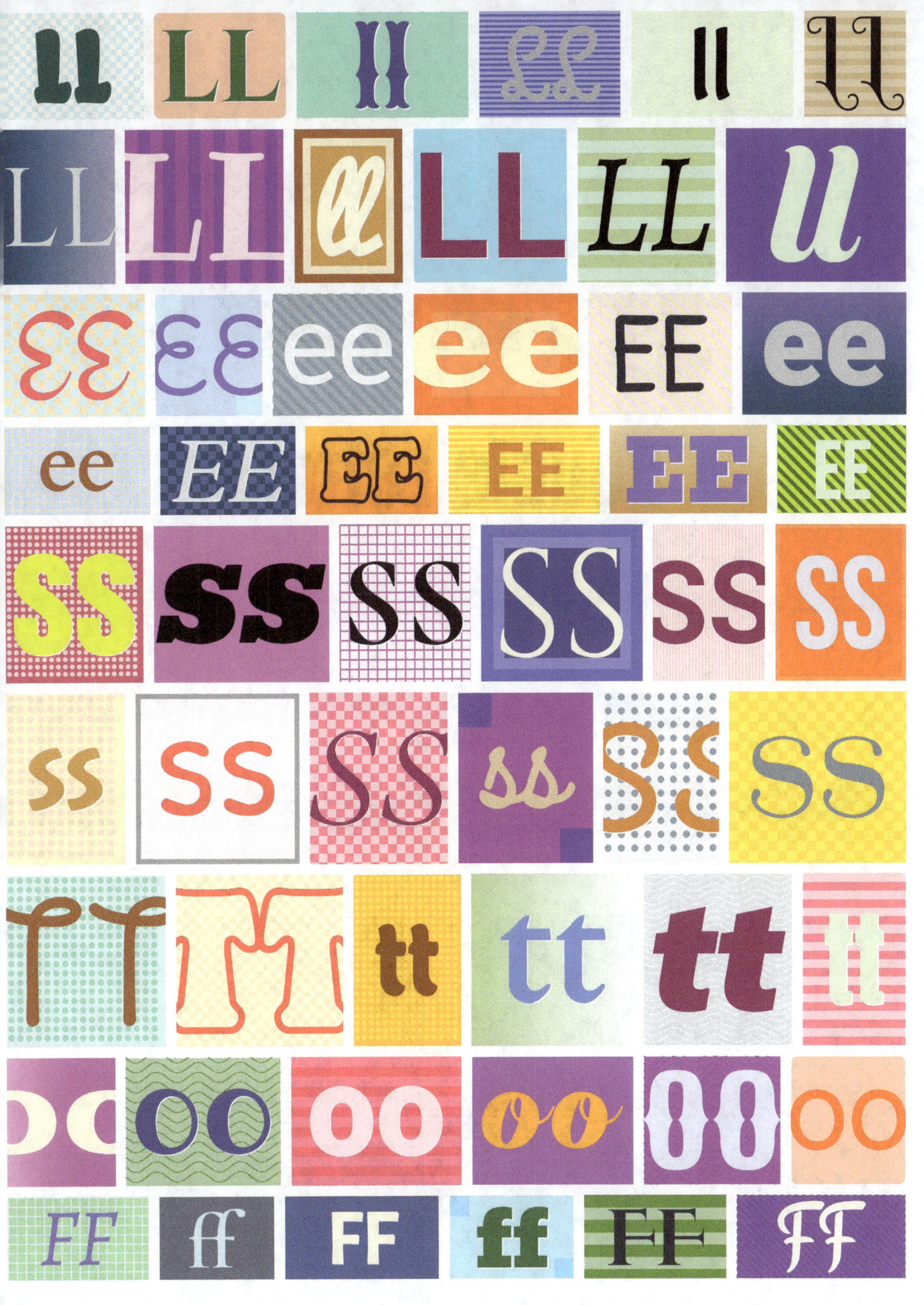

Double Letters

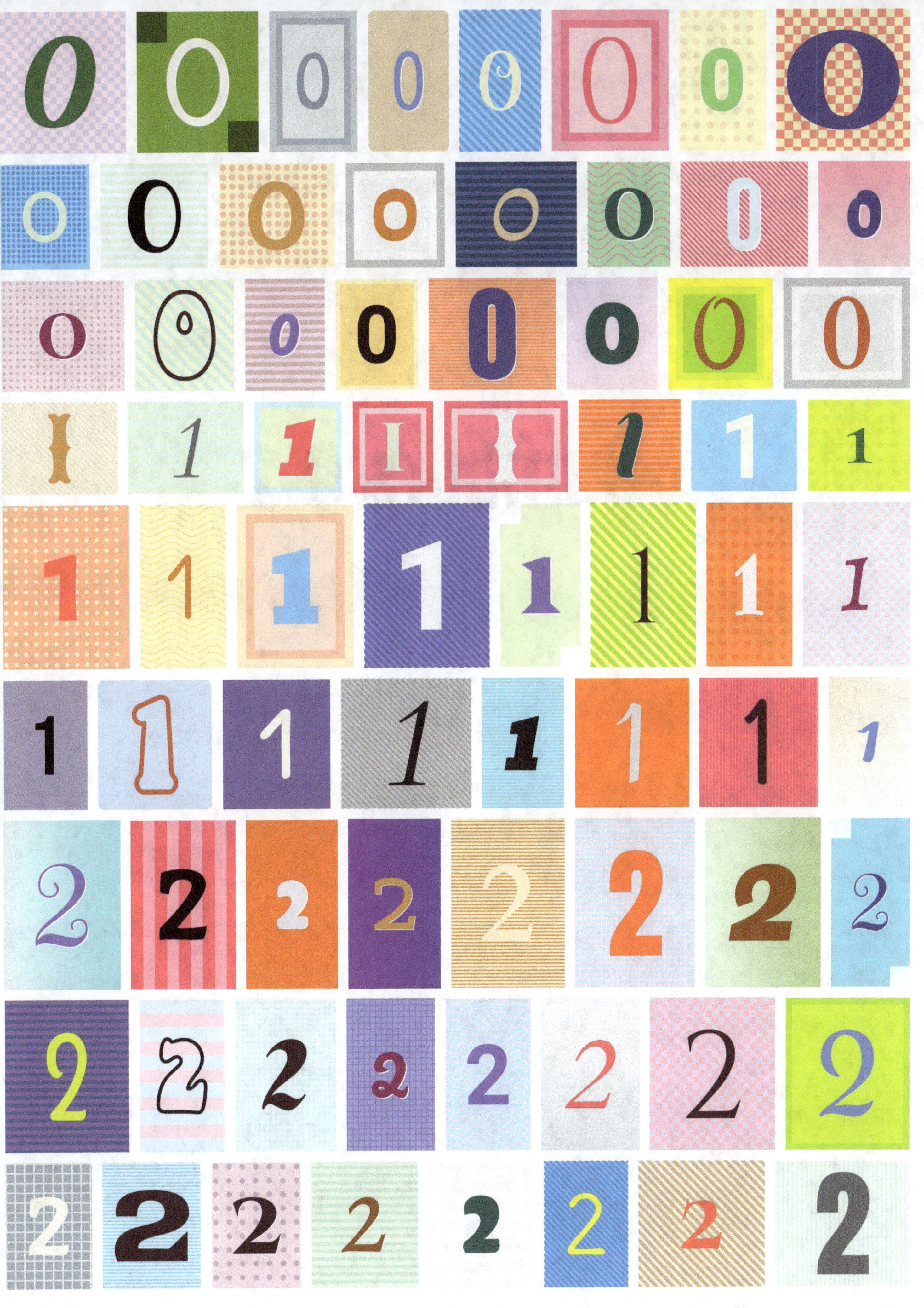

Numbers 0-2

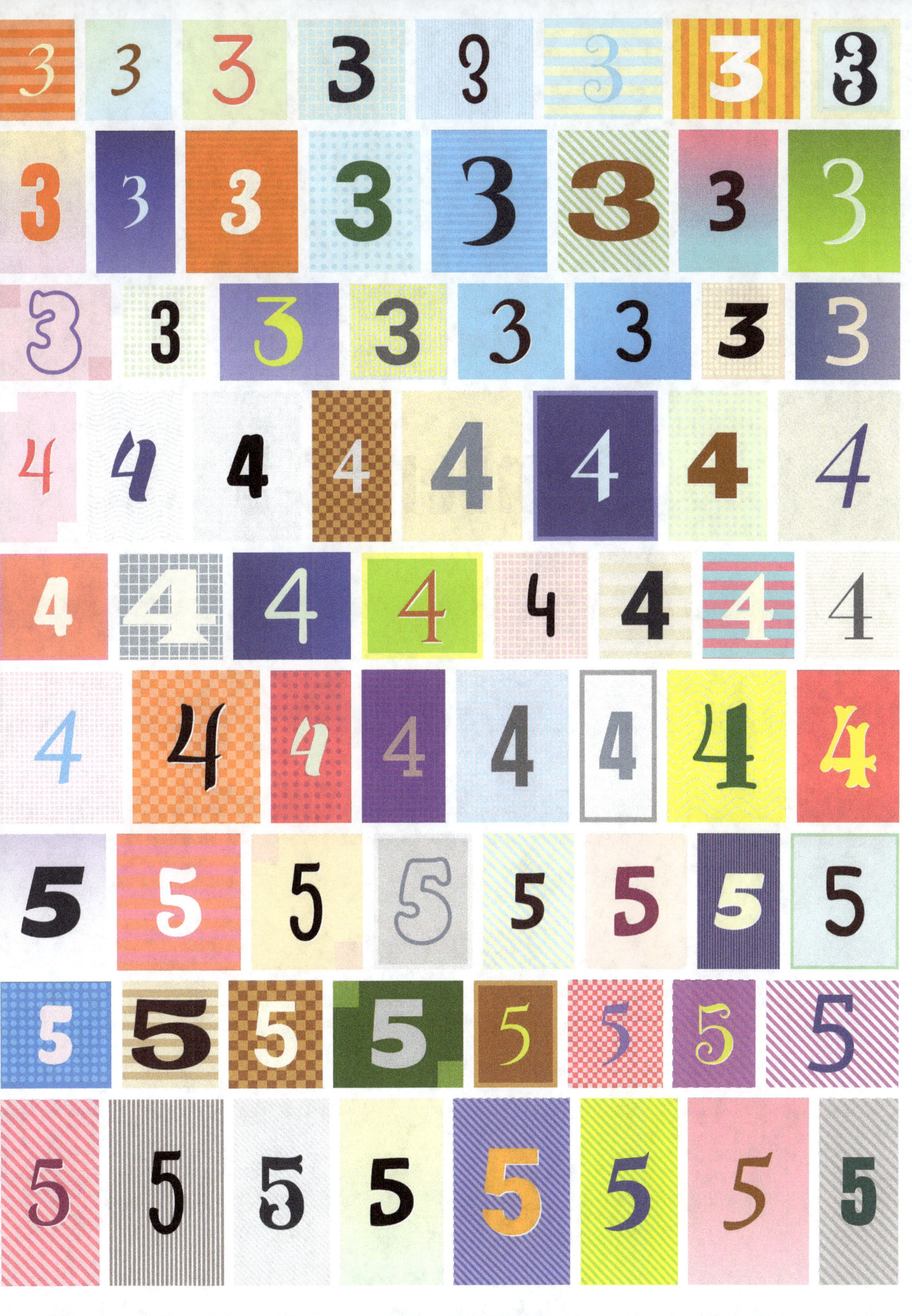

Numbers 3-5

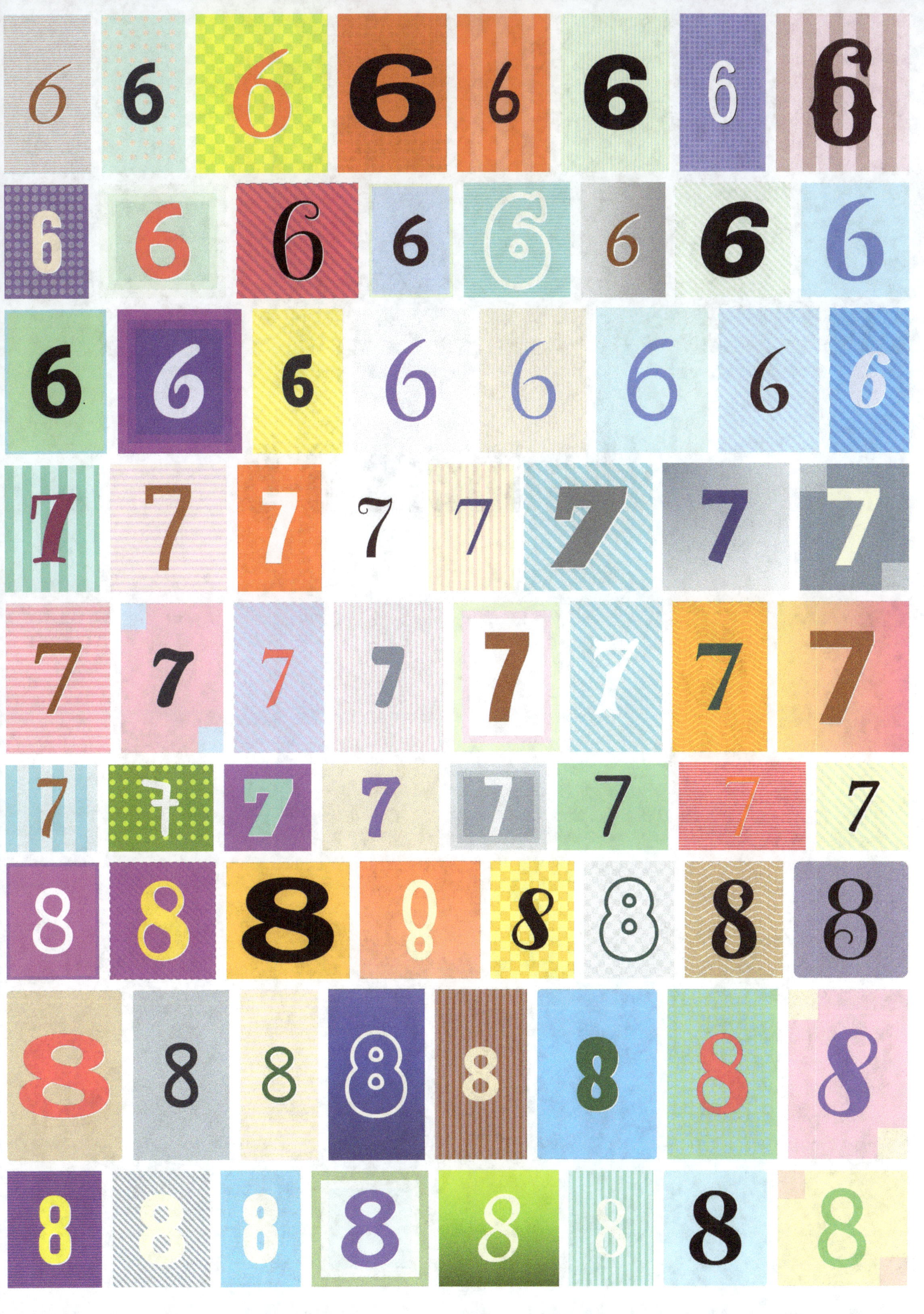

Numbers 6-8

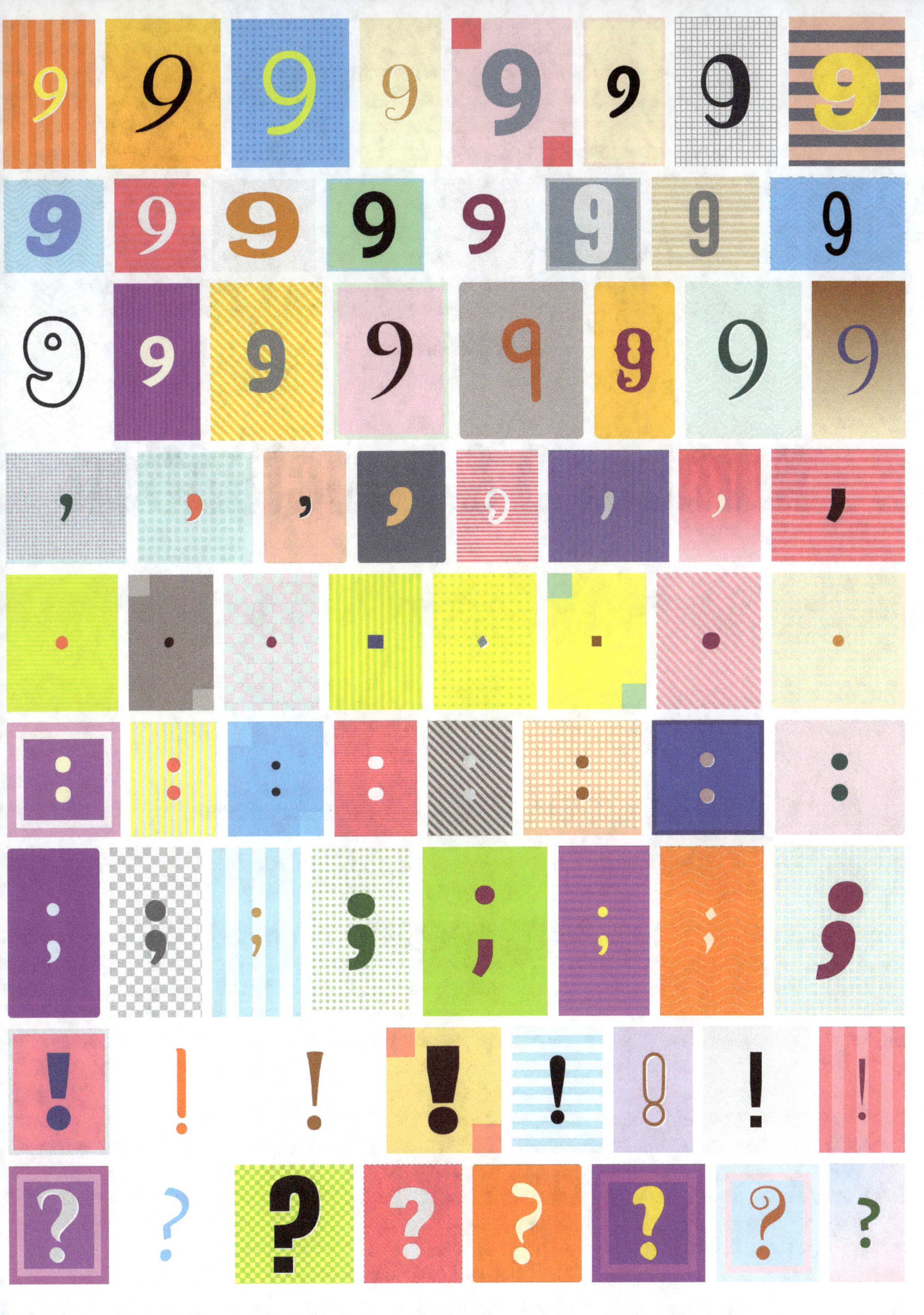

Number 9 & Punctuation

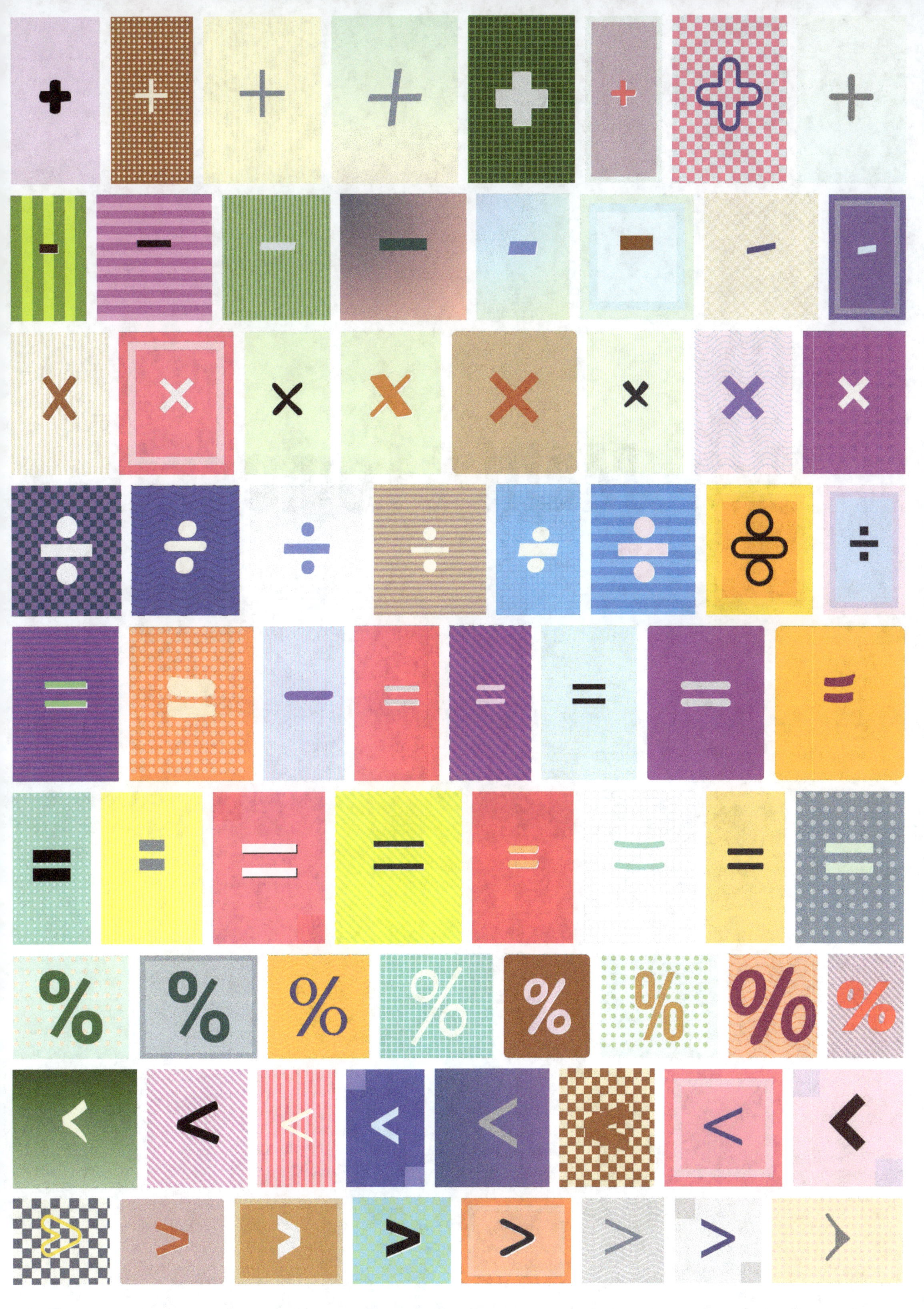

Math & Logic

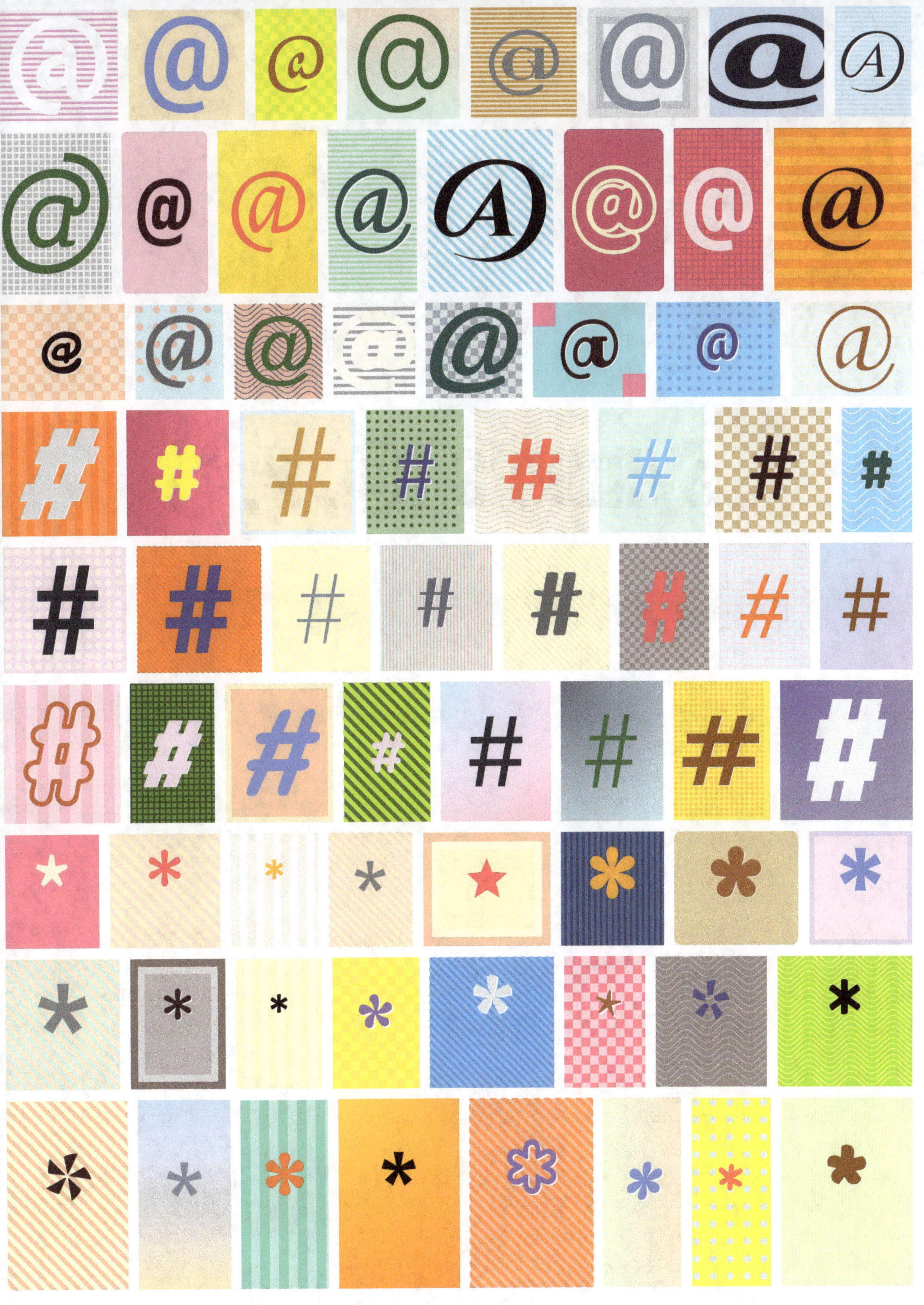

Symbols (@, #, *)

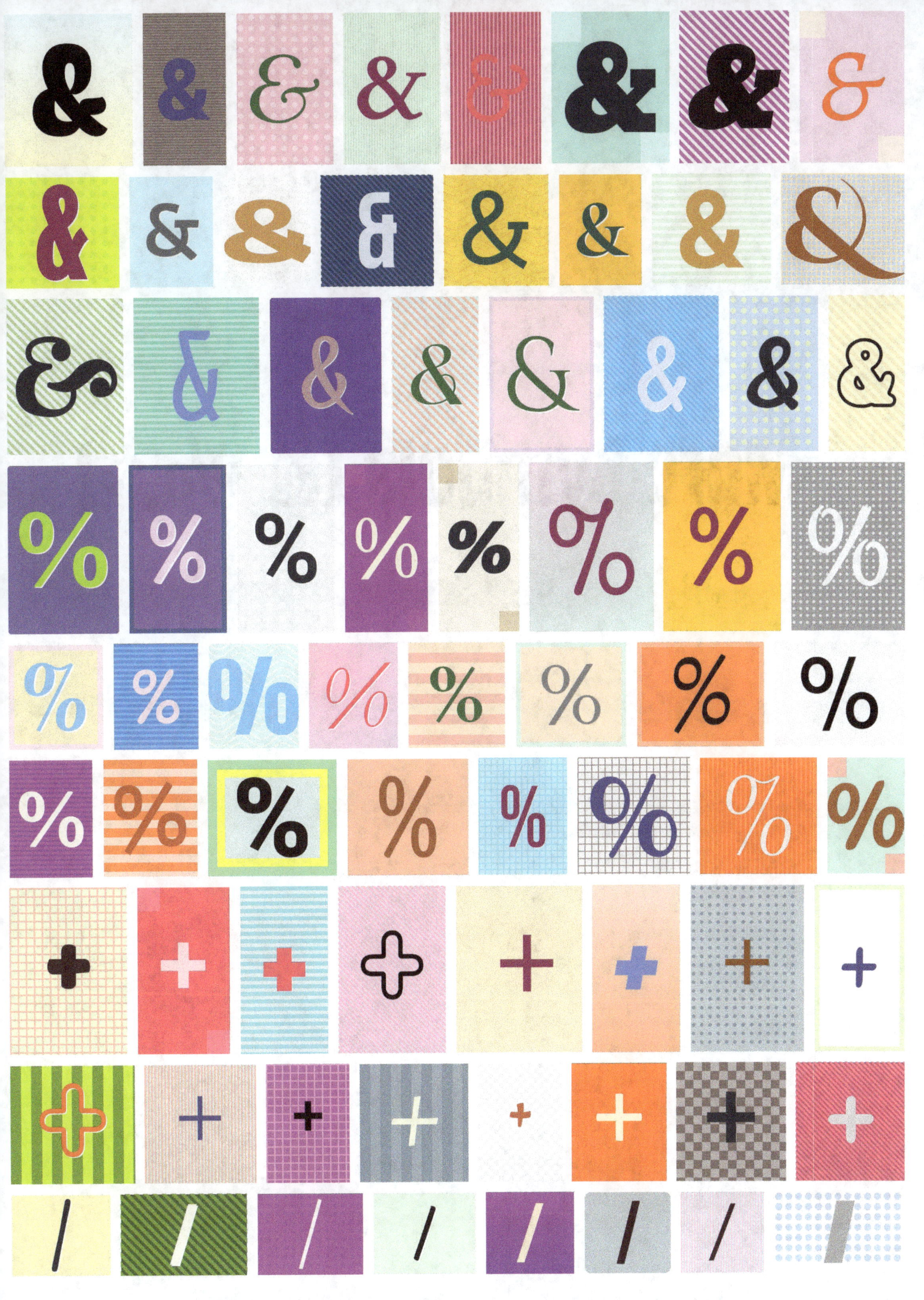

More Symbols (&, %, +)

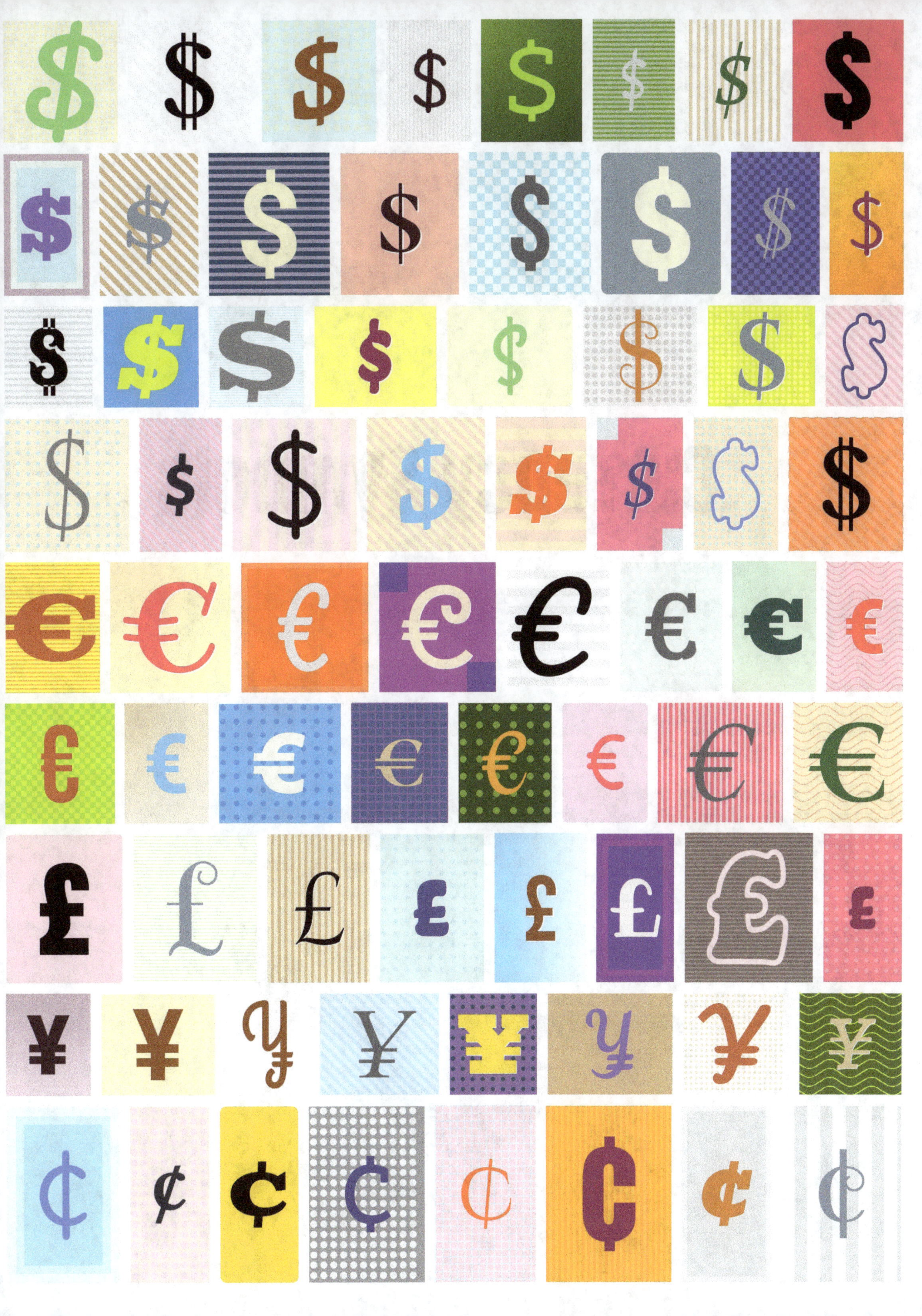

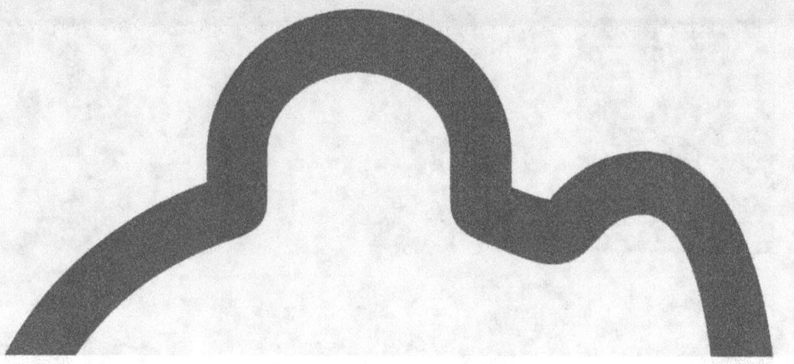

Currency Symbols

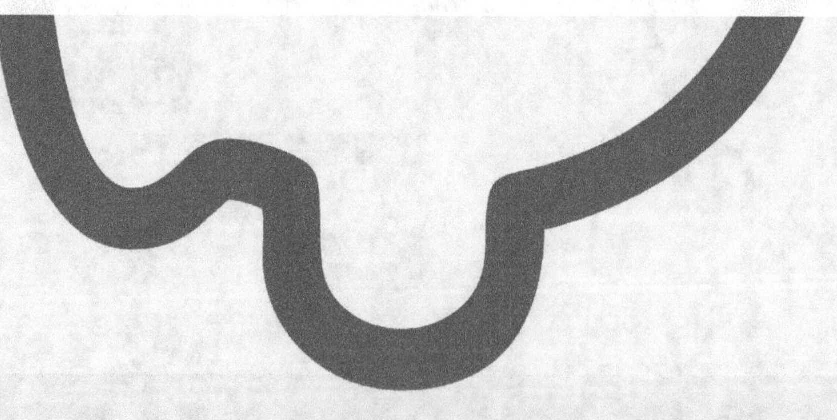

the the THE

the THE THE

AND AND AND

AND AND and

for for FOR

YOU you YOU

ARE are are

WAS was WAS

BUT but but

Common Words

mon mon mon

MON mon MON

tue tue TUE

WED WED wed

THU THU THU

fri FRI FRI

SAT sat sat

SUN sun sun

sun SUN sun

Days of the Week

JAN jan jan

JAN JAN jan

feb FEB feb

mar mar mar

apr apr APR

MAY MAY MAY

jun jun JUN

JAN JAN jan

FEB feb FEB

Months (Jan-Jun)

JUL   jul   jul

JUL   JUL   jul

aug   aug   AUG

sep   sep   sep

OCT   OCT   OCT

NOV   NOV   NOV

dec   dec   DEC

JUL   JUL   JUL

aug   aug   aug

Months (Jul-Dec)